In the Footsteps of Walker Women

Helen Aitchison

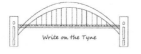

Write on the Tyne Publishing

ISBN: 978-1-7394882-1-5
Write on the Tyne Publishing

Cover design by Write on the Tyne
Image: istiockphoto.com

*To all the women of Walker;
past, present, and future. May
we always remember your
stories and may we always
walk in your footsteps.*

Foreword

By Christine Carroll, Pottery Bank Community Centre

Walker is a residential suburb and electoral ward in the south-east of Newcastle upon Tyne. It spans the area between Welbeck Road and the banks of the River Tyne. Pottery Bank is a small area within Walker which follows the current of the River Tyne from west to east. Its name derives from one of the earliest industries in the area, the pottery industry which was first established between 1780 and 1790. Pottery was produced in this area for two centuries.

In 1853 Christopher Thompson Maling (1824-1901) took over the running of the Ouseburn Bridge Pottery from his father Robert. By 1859 the two kilns at the Ouseburn Bridge works were unable to cope with the demand, and a new pottery was built on a site known as the Ford Pottery (later the Ford A Pottery). From thirteen kilns it produced 750,000 items a month. Later a huge new pottery was built at Walker, the Ford B Pottery, completed in 1878. For almost fifty years the two Ford Potteries employed between them over a thousand workers, with the Ford B Pottery turning out over 1,500,000 items a month.

What made Maling unusual for a Tyneside firm was the large number of women they employed. The Maling workforce was predominantly female. The women operated machinery and, at times, carried heavy loads on their backs. They also made up teams of artists who decorated the items of china that were produced. The women were known as "white mice," because they were covered in china dust at the end of their shift. C. T. Maling and Sons as a business closed in 1963.

The world of work in the North East until well into the twentieth century was very heavily gendered. The main industries were coal mining and shipbuilding where a large proportion of the men worked. The women were needed and expected to be at home to cook, wash and clean for their husbands and sons; very few were able to take on paid work outside the home. The idea that "A woman's place is in the home" prevailed well into the 1980s.

With the closing of coal mines and shipyards came the challenges of unemployment in the area. If her husband was unable to find suitable work then the woman often found work for herself.

In Jane Austen's novel, Northanger Abbey, the main character, Catherine Morland complained that she didn't care for history, where she found

'Hardly any women at all – it's very tiresome.' Women's lives have been affected by every aspect of history and social change, yet their voices have frequently been absent from discussions.

Women learn informally from mothers and grandmothers – skills, knowledge and often attitudes. Whilst there is always change, there is also continuity among the changes:

'The past in the present, the carrying from generation to generation of values and attitudes.' (Dr Maureen Callcott; 'A Woman's Place', 1999).

Our stories are connected – between generations. Part of our present story is made up of our past experiences and also the experiences and recollections that others have shared. This is all part of our heritage.

The stories and contributions in this book form part of our ongoing heritage, not only our personal heritage but also the shared heritage of our community and of women everywhere. We all have stories to tell, experiences to share; we all have voices.

You're not on your own here – it's like a big family. You can have an argument with someone one day, leave her and go and see someone else; by the time you see that person again, they've forgotten about it! The place is big enough for that, but small enough to know lots of people.

We've lived all over and done all sorts. O hinny, we've lived! But we could tell stories every day for a month about Pottery Bank and there'd still be more.

Everybody is a story. In telling our stories we are telling each other a small part of the universal human story to which we can all relate.

Contents

When people tell us their story,
we are to hold it as delicately
as a flower with as much
honour and respect.

Lillian Lake

Independent Women

My first home in Newcastle was in Fairless Street, Byker. I was born in 1954 into a flat that was our family home until I was 12 years old. The house was tiny, with one bedroom, living room, and scullery. As our family grew, I can recall my mother visiting the council one day to enquire about a larger house for us all. She came back gobsmacked that the council had advised her to have a bigger family due to not scoring enough points to access council housing as a smaller family!

I had two siblings, both brothers. My eldest brother, Ken, was born when I was about five years old, followed by David, five years later. It wasn't easy and understandably stressful for my parents who tried hard to ensure we all had a bed and space. In the back yard, we had a steel bath that was hung up on the wall. Bath day was a Friday. We would fill up the bath then patiently wait our turn, hoping that the water wasn't cold by the time it came to our wash and wishing perhaps a little more that the water wasn't too manky! Baths certainly weren't a luxury when you were last in the queue and had to clean yourself in dirty water. We had a pull-down bed and my youngest brother used to sleep in a cot in the living room. We had a black range in the house where my mother made the fire up each day. She would cook in the oven and on cold mornings, she would put our clothes out to warm by the fire or oven. In those days we didn't have central heating but it was always lovely to get into the toasty clothes as Mam looked on, a smile on her face. With what we had, we made a lovely family and we were never short of love.

Me as a young girl   Dad with a family friend

Dad worked on the railways and my mother was a housewife when we were younger then worked part-time, including at Greggs the bakery. Poverty was almost normal in those days. People did without a lot of things and made do with so many others. We were the original recyclers – nothing got wasted and everything had a purpose. We had to. It was survival and life was hard for a large amount of people. Our flat was part of the slum houses in the area, that were demolished many years ago. A deprived community but we never felt deprived and I had a positive childhood with fond memories of playing in the back lane where we lived. It was our little community within a community, a daily adventure. Our small back yard would be jam-packed with items and children! There was an outside toilet, a coal shed, a rabbit hutch, and an air raid shelter. Yet it was the place to be and our back yard became like the local youth club, us all piling in and the air filled with laughter, playing and being kids!

I remember having a desk and chair that was bought by my aunt and grandma. I loved it and although it was probably given to do school work from, I would sit at it in the back yard and the local children would sit in lines in front of the desk and chair as I sat there, like a queen on her throne, playing teacher! I would write in exercise books and teach them about certain topics and subjects. Then we would play pretend hospitals where all the kids would lie in a makeshift bed and we would go around imitating using a stethoscope and thermometer. The "medicine" administered was usually a Swizzels sweet.

Our childhood had a beauty that involved us being able to make our own fun. We weren't bored kids because we used our imagination and created games, adventure, and laughs ourselves. In the summer holidays, Mam would give us a bottle of water and a bag of jam sandwiches. We would head off as a group of kids to Byker Park and spend the whole day there. We would make dens in the vicarage, run around, and play hide and seek. We would climb the rocks, pretending they were mountains and move around the park using our minds to entertain ourselves. A firm favourite was picking a flower and licking the petals before placing them on our nails as nail varnish! We would spend hours doing this and loved it. Another activity involved us standing by the bowling green, picking at the privet and lattice working it through the fences. The parkkeeper would look out for us, checking we weren't misbehaving too much. Great memories in a time when kids could be kids – carefree and with a focus on friendship and fun.

Above our flat, an elderly couple lived. Every night I would go up to their flat and fill their coal bucket up and ask if they had any messages or needed anything from the corner shop. This was another role we all had in the community – to look after our older citizens. I would wait and see if the old couple would perhaps give me a penny for my help. However, I always got the same message,

'Thanks very much for this, pet. I'll dance at your wedding!'

It makes me smile now. He never did dance at my wedding, passing before that and I never did get a penny for running errands.

Washing day in the street was the same day for everyone and my mam was the first person to get a

Hotpoint washing machine. In those days, you were judged on the cleanliness of your washing, especially your net curtains and keeping your doorstep clean. All the parents in the street knew one another. There was a strong community feeling, a sense of solidarity and if anyone needed something, they only had to knock on their neighbour's door. No one had anything, but they always had something to share, even if it was just words of comfort. Kindness like that cost nothing and kept the heartbeat of our street going. Families during that time lived nearby to one another, often in the same street or next door to one another. Childcare was taken care of and I used to go to my grandma's for tea after school before my aunt brought me back home. We were all close and neighbours became additional "Auntie's and Uncle's." The community was small, with everything we needed in a close parameter including the shops, doctors, and school. Everyone and everything was familiar. Great for support but not so great if you got into trouble!

Within the community, there was psychological support that you wouldn't get now. I remember being a small child and there was a lady called Mrs. Harkness who lived a few doors down from us. She had a son called Gordan, who was a lovely man and the community loved him. He tragically died young and I can remember the devastation felt by the whole street as grief soaked the air. The local women gave Mrs. Harkness support by sitting with her all night, each taking turns. I'm not sure if that would happen now, but it went on for a while after the tragedy and every woman in the street offered help. It feels like the community never forgot one another. Despite being busy and life being hard, they still had time for each other.

Auntie Jean and Grandma   Grandma and Auntie Amy

The streets were full of characters and I remember one fondly. She was called Mrs. Ashcroft. Her husband had a coal merchant on the back lane and they also had a newsagent. Due to their businesses, they had a lot more money than most people in the area. I remember Mrs. Ashcroft as she was somewhat of a pioneer in those days. She was bold, beautiful, and powerful. Mrs. Ashcroft had bright red hair and wore a leopard print coat. In addition to this, she would wear lots of gold jewellery and high-heeled shoes. She was like a film star and her presence would make us all stop and look up, mesmerised. She challenged the gender expectations and roles of the time that women were homemakers, "looked" like mothers and housewives, didn't go out on their own, and answered to their husbands and the men in society. Mrs. Ashcroft was independent and formidable. I learnt a lot of lessons from her and part of me really wanted to be like her when I grew up.

There was another lady in the street who was very different to Mrs. Ashcroft. While Mrs. Ashcroft was the in light, this lady was in darkness. She was a victim of domestic abuse, disrespected, downtrodden, and controlled. I remember one time her husband beat her so badly that her eye socket was broken and her eye looked like it was falling out. My mam went to help, that time and on other occasions. We all knew what happened in her household but she never left her abusive husband. Seeing her and then the complete opposite in Mrs. Ashcroft, I knew the type of life I wanted.

All of the women in my family were independent to a degree. Many of them worked; my aunt worked in Parsons and my grandma worked at the General Hospital. Mam's parents had passed but they used to own properties and had a corner shop, so my late grandma had worked. Mam worked part-time so a work ethic was drummed into me. The women in my family had a sense of their place in the world and were positive role models. Perhaps not as bold as Mrs. Ashcroft, who was the anomaly in those days, but working women were an important group in challenging roles. So many women at that time "knew their place" and would remain in the home, never working and instead cleaning the house, bringing the kids up. They had limited independence and identity, relying on the male breadwinner. Of course, many women were happy with this and it doesn't make it wrong, but I knew I wanted to be like the women in my life and those before me. I wanted to be an independent woman.

Byker and Walker had a lot of local industry during my childhood, including railways and shipbuilding. Men would have dirty jobs but one lovely thing about both men and women in those days was their clothes and even with little items and money, they would make the effort to look smart and get dressed up outside of work. It was an important part of their identity. People had two lives, one working long hours, in a hard industry and another getting dressed up and spending time with their families or going to local dances. People were strong-minded and had a massive sense of pride in themselves, their families, and their communities.

We had events throughout the year that brought the whole community together. Bonfire night was an example. You might not have seen someone for the full year but you would see them on Bonfire night as the whole lane got together. It wasn't always about the actual event, but the idea of everyone coming together, connecting as a community. It was a special thing. When the streets around Fairless Street were demolished, many of the families moved to Walker streets together. It meant the closeness and the friendships moved with them.

Auntie Amy (front left) and work friends from the ropery, Wallsend

Dad

When I was 12 years old we moved to Morley Street on Heaton Road. I remember myself and my middle brother going into the house and seeing the inside bath. We were astonished, never having seen one before. Like people visiting abroad for the first time, it was amazing! We stood and turned the taps on and off for about ten minutes, squealing with excitement at the thought of a bath that didn't have to be lugged into the house from outside and painstakingly filled over and over with water that seemed to evaporate. The new house was a rented flat and we all had our own room. Then a few years later when I was 15 years old, we secured a council house on Winslow Close in Walker, which at the time was a new estate. I remained in the family home until I was 19 years old when I got married and moved over to Wallsend.

My school in Walker was Victoria Jubilee School and I enjoyed my education. It was very traditional and my dad had also studied at this school. I took my 11+ and interestingly, for the 11+, the boys had a lower threshold to obtain a pass than the girls. It was a big thing to pass the 11+, especially in our community which was seen as deprived. After these exams, genders were separated and I was moved to the Technical School for Girls. I enjoyed this school - it was like Harry Potter with our uniforms and the old-fashioned teachers, whose lives had been dedicated to teaching the girls. When I was 15 years old and still at school, the Labour government at the time changed the way exams would occur, deciding that all the schools would be comprehensive. This meant that all of a sudden the whole system changed and our school was amalgamated with the secondary modern schools, alongside the boy's school. The teachers couldn't cope, it was a massive change to their years of teaching and routine. We went from a small, all-girls school to a large, mixed-gender school. Hormones were shooting off like fireworks and who fancied who quickly became more important than exams! The statistics for that year demonstrated the impact of this and resulted in the lowest exam rate and move-on stats. The school became as chaotic as the Boxing Day sales, with kids fighting, boisterous lessons, and teachers having breakdowns. I hated it.

At the time, I was working a Saturday job at a hairdressing salon on Shields Road in Byker. I went in one Saturday during Easter and asked if there were any jobs going, desperate to leave school. I was offered an apprentice role and it was when Shields Road was up and coming, the place to be, so it suited me just fine. The place was thriving and I did my apprenticeship, earning £1.75 per week. However, I used to get plenty of tips so it was wonderful having money. I decided I didn't like hairdressing in the end as I didn't enjoy the weekend working, especially as I was spending most of my weekends out at the clubs such as The Oxford Galleries in Newcastle. We would also frequent The Pineapple, The Chain Locker, and The Swallow Hotel. I remember one time in 1969, going to The Swallow Hotel for the first time with my cousin, who was also an apprentice. We were young and not the legal age to be in bars but we had dressed up and styled our hair like the other hairdressers, trying to look older than our years. I recall we got there and went down the stairs to the bar and looked in. Glancing around, everyone had long hair, wore glasses and was dressed in hippy-style clothing. We would have stood out like a purple giraffe had we gone in. Instead, we trundled back up the stairs, annoyed with ourselves but returned the weekend after in hippy-style clothing!

I was 17 years old when I met my husband, Michael. I had been out in Newcastle, planning to meet a date who had stood me up. Walking up Dean Street, I was livid that the guy hadn't turned up. In my own little world, I continued up the street shaking my head. Across the road, I heard voices and looked over to see a man pointing at me.

'That's the girl you've been tapping up in the Red House.' He said, jabbing his friend and nodding my way.

I stopped and they crossed the road, convinced this girl was me. I was heading off to a party in another part of the city, following my date no-show. They stood next to me and I thought I quite fancied one of them! He told me his name was Michael, shortened to Mick and I casually asked him if he wanted to come to a party, shrugging my shoulders. He gave a big smile before telling me he would love to then off we went. And we have partied together ever since! Mick and I have been married for 50 years. When we met, he lived in Denton Hall, which was the polar opposite of where I was from. I remember taking Mick home to meet my family and Mam asked him what he did for a living. At the time he was a trainee architectural technician and he was spoilt by my mam who saw he was a decent lad who had focus and a future, perfect for her only daughter.

Mick and me on our wedding day

As a couple, Mick and me moved to Wallsend when I was 19 years old, after getting married. I remember my mother talking about us having a white wedding at church, as she was Catholic and me knowing I wouldn't be doing that. I wanted to get married at the Civic Centre, in Newcastle, despite all the family expecting me to have a big, white wedding. Instead, I chose a red wedding dress with the Civic Centre as our venue. When I announced Mick and me were to be wed, I told my mam it would be in six weeks. She was aghast with the rush and the community thought I was pregnant. I wasn't, I had just fallen in love. We wanted to get married and then move into our flat in Wallsend that we planned to rent for £5 per week. Our wedding was small, followed by a meal at The Rainbow Room in the Co-op and a party at Mick's mam's house. It was brilliant, no fuss, no pressure.

As we were married young I wanted us to enjoy married life and we were married 13 years before we had our only child, Laura. I had seen so many women with three or four children by their late 20s. I didn't want that and we didn't have Laura until I was 32 years old. Sadly, by this time my mam had died. She passed when she was just 50 years old and I was 25 years old, so she never got the chance to meet our daughter. Laura is now in her 30s and is an amazing, strong, beautiful woman. Dad carried on after Mam died and moved out of the family home to the Midway in Walker. Ken had joined the RAF and David stayed in the Midway, housed opposite my dad for all the time he lived there. Dad ended up in elderly care and passed around ten years ago.

During my career, I had several jobs and a strong work ethic was instilled in me by my family. In the very early 1970s we had the experience of full employment in that you could finish a job on the

Friday, attend the Jobcentre the following Monday and be interviewed and start in a new company the next week. It was quick and there was a choice. One place I worked was Peacocks Medical Supplies then in around 1985 computers arrived! I worked in Wallsend in a place called Metano. My role was in the office getting involved with the new phenomena of technology.

My Auntie Amy, Laura, and me.

When I moved to North Shields, I worked all my jobs on Howard Street, a walkable distance. My career finished in 2020 in a local accountancy company. For the last 14 years, I was working in payroll mainly. When I was 63 years old, I became worried about keeping up at work so I left the firm and found another job with a local business for a few days a week, before retiring in 2020. The pandemic then hit and I agreed to help with some elements as the company was in the care sector. I have continued to help out now and then if needed as they are a great organisation.

Since retiring, I'm very active. I go to the YMCA gym in North Shields and I enjoy writing and going to a writing group. I paint and find both art and writing therapeutic. Mick and I have travelled and continue to, we have visited amazing countries and cities such as New York and Paris. We have been very lucky. I adore my retirement after working for 51 years and I try and make the most of each day.

Me with a piece of my artwork

Byker and Walker will always hold a special place in my heart. I can look back and see how women have changed over the years and the importance of the voice of women, that even as a child I recognised and aimed for. Women were strong in many ways, but society and expectations often tried to silence them. It frequently worked, but not always. Byker and Walker was my childhood home and shaped me into the adult I became. It's my history. Precious memories of family, community, and friendship were rooted into the streets there. It was the cement between the bricks that were used to build the houses of the community's residents. And even though many were demolished long ago, the memories remain and if people are lucky, the cement still keeps families and friends together.

Pauline Sheldon, aged 68.

Dedicated to my auntie Amy.

Vitalite Nights

I was born in Byker in the mid-1980s, a time that felt like a good era to be a kid. Growing up in the 1980s and early 1990s, life was all about fun and friendship and we didn't have the pressures children have these days. I have two older brothers, David and Stephen, who were protective. Sometimes they would babysit and they always caught spiders for me, even though they admitted when they were older that they were scared of them as well! The three of us were brought up by my mam as a single parent. I saw my dad, who lived in Pelaw but it was just us four at home and Mam did an amazing job of raising us.

I went to St Lawrence's School in Byker. School was school and I never had any problems, enjoying it on the whole. I loved home time as this meant playing out time in the street with my friends. We would play "tuggy" and hide and seek. We would dance and do gymnastics, like handstands and cartwheels. Life was carefree and every day felt like the beginning of a new opportunity for fun, the way it should be for kids. We would all play out, getting along and then Mam would call me in for tea. I was always determined to stay out longer, savouring every minute of playing out in all weathers with my friends. In the summer, days would last forever as we played in the back lane. It felt like our own adventure film as our squeals of delight and laughter carried away with the summer breeze.

Mam used to make homemade chips, that always tasted fantastic. The fluffy potato soaked in vinegar, they were one of my favourites. I used to plead to have my food outside, not wanting to come in and for the fun to stop. Mam would pile my chips into an old Vitalite margarine tub, instead of a plate that would no doubt end up getting smashed outside. Somehow the chips always seemed to taste even better in that Vitalite tub!

Me as a youngster

As I got a little older I loved music and each week I would get the magazine Smash Hits! It would have the words of the latest chart-topping songs from bands I liked such as The Backstreet Boys, that

I could rip out and sing along as the charts played each Sunday. There would be posters of singers and actors, the latest heartthrobs, to display on your door and wall. I would watch Wizadora and Tots TV, and watch Beetlejuice over and over on VHS then DVD. Life was good with many happy memories.

I remember the old dial-up AOL Internet and the piercing noise it used to make whilst waiting to connect. It would drone on for what felt like forever until we could "surf the web." We were never allowed on for long as it made the home landline engaged so no one could get through if they were ringing. It was usually an hour here and there I was allocated and ten minutes of that would be absorbed by the connection time!

When I was 11 years old, I went to senior school. It was tolerable but in some ways I rebelled a little. I used to go to Sea Cadets after school, twice a week which I loved. If I had been naughty, Mam would tell me I couldn't go, which would break my heart – it was a massive part of my life at the time and a place where I felt I learnt but also entertained me. We would learn boating, knots, target practice, and teamwork. It was somewhere I made friends, built confidence, and felt part of a big quest.

I remember as a youngster I wanted to be a nurse. Mam was a nurse and I always admired her desire to help other people. She seemed to be forever making people's lives better, easier, and more comfortable. Then she would return home and look after us. She was amazing and still is. However, nothing came of my desire and I left school at 16 years old. My first job was working at KFC and I worked there for around eight years. It was a great job and the team made it, they were lovely people. Then I met my partner, Mark when I was 18 years old. We met on a night out and he was also local, from Fenham. When we became official, he moved over to Walker and we are still together. We had our first child, our daughter, Amy, when I was 21 years old. Ryan followed five years later.

Amy is 15 years old and Ryan is 10 years old. They are great kids but I see a lot of change from when I was younger. There is a real generational difference in a lot of ways and I'm certain my mam also sees this when comparing my childhood and her grandchildren's. Technology and the reliance on it by the younger generation is a massive difference from when I was growing up. It's as if their world ends if their phone battery goes or they can't get on the iPad! Also, the way they play now, there's no use of imagination. Everything is provided for kids through the Internet. The brain isn't used to create much, to imagine and to make their own fun.

A major change from my childhood is that kids these days don't play out on the streets like we did. It feels less safe and for that reason, staying in the house could be a good thing. But it feels like a shame. We used to be out all day and night, playing, running around, exercising and laughing! Using our imagination. We would be exhausted by the end of the night from running around, enjoying the fresh air and nature around us. We would go to bed shattered but happy and excited for the next day to play. It felt like the world was a big playground and I don't think we ever got bored. Precious times being innocent children. Kids today sit behind a screen, talking to robots or people online through apps. No imagination and no exercise. I would struggle to let my kids out now, it's a scary world. Hearing of stabbings and gang violence. Perhaps crime has always gone on and I was shielded as a child but now, as a parent, I read about it and see it and need to protect my family.

My daughter has never been one to play out and my son just plays in the car park at the back. He wouldn't go wandering and I wouldn't let him. The kids know most of the dangers of society and are streetwise. As necessary as that is, it feels sad. But they have to be aware as there are predators everywhere, a danger on every street corner and darkness waiting to dull the light of childhood. Children also seem to have so much pressure now. We didn't have to worry about what we wore, what we had, and who we were going to play with. Now kids have to fit in and if not bullying comes from all angles, including online. It's cruel and sad. Kids grow up quicker than they should. Innocence shattered like a light bulb falling to the ground.

Me with my friend, Linda and Mam, Christine

Me, Mam, and Linda

Women's roles have also changed over the years, even in my time. Women seem to be more empowered and it's a great thing. I hope as my daughter gets older, this continues and that future generations of women have more choices, breaking out of gender stereotypes. I hope women have continued opportunity and there aren't the expectations of being a housewife, cleaning, and cooking or being a mother and having no other identity. There has to be chance, opportunity, and equality. I've felt this in my adulthood, compared to my mother for example, and I hope my daughter feels it more as the years pass.

The community here in Walker is good and I have neighbours who I know would help if I needed them and likewise, I would offer support back. We are all perhaps more reserved and less friendly than in the past when doors were left open and everyone knew each other and their business. Reluctance, fear, or just being too busy with our own lives, I'm not sure. Some people on your street you will never say more than a hello to but as long as there are some close people and that sense of community, because it does matter. Pottery Bank Community Centre is a big part of that sense of community in the area. It's something that provides support, activities, and advice for all ages and for every family, regardless. We attend the well-being groups with my friends and family. It's also nice that I have something for me as an individual where I can be Kristine. I've met new people, made friends, and learnt new skills. We've done crafts and exercise such as chair yoga. We have a good laugh and sometimes we just come and you don't have to say a word, you can sit and get involved with an activity or you can just sit and be. Everyone is accepted and it feels like a comfy pair of slippers.

Kristine Allen, aged 37.

Dedicated to my family.

Finding Home

I've lived in Walker for almost 20 years but spent the first 30 years of my life in Islington, London. I'm of West Indian heritage, my dad being Jamaican and my mum being from Barbados. Childhood was a time of happy memories that I cherish. Growing up in the 1970s in London, I learnt a lot about my heritage as well as the multicultural communities of London. It was a place of friendship, safety, and acceptance with Mum teaching me Caribbean cooking and hair braiding, which I still do today and have passed the tradition onto my daughter.

Mum was a single parent, bringing me and four younger sister's up. Six females in a house made for a hive of activity! I'm the oldest and there are around four years between each of us, my youngest sister being in her mid-30s now. We didn't see much of my dad growing up and as I was the oldest, I helped Mum out with the childcare and keeping our home. I have a precious memory of Mum teaching me how to braid hair at the age of five years old. We were sitting in the bed together as I held my little rag doll, named Sarah. She demonstrated on Sarah how to braid hair and I could braid my own hair by the age of eight years old. It was my first job when I was around 12 years old, getting pocket money for braiding our neighbour's and Mum's friend's hair. A young entrepreneur! Mum was on benefits and sometimes it was hard, the six of us all needing and wanting a never-ending list of items. Braiding gave me a little bit of pocket money that helped towards buying things, as well as sharing the wonderful skill Mum had taught me.

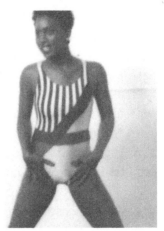

Me and my sister, London (1983)

Me, aged 16

Growing up in Islington, I have fond memories of school. I loved art and continued to develop my artistic skills through secondary school and in higher education, studying art, sociology and English literature at A-level. After this, I completed a foundation degree in art and felt fashion design could be a good area for me to focus on. I remember making garments and producing items for a fashion show. At this time, I was applying for placements at some art colleges in London, including Goldsmiths College of Art. It was a real dream of mine but soon the paint bubble burst and I realised that perhaps it was more challenging to achieve a career in the art world that would allow me to make a living. It could be a hobby but I soon realised not having any connections in the art world meant it was unlikely to ever offer a sustainable income as a job.

Some of my early artwork

I had always been employed since leaving school. My first main job was in Waitrose on the deli counter, where I worked for seven years. Alongside work, I was involved with things in the community, such as Sure Start, including being part of their board of governors. I had a small flat in Islington with my partner before I fell pregnant with my daughter, Nazarene (Naz). Her father and I chose her name as I was told I wouldn't be able to have children due to a medical condition, polycystic ovaries. I was around 28 years old and was exploring IVF treatment, when we discovered I was pregnant. I felt it was like a miracle and we had been blessed by God with this baby. We looked through The Bible for a name and Nazarene stood out. So that was where our daughter's name was found. Our miracle.

Our flat, where I had lived for ten years in Islington, was one-bedroomed with no lift. The area was Jeremy Corbyn's constituency and I had visited Jeremy a few times at his surgery. The block of flats we lived in had problems – the estate was a social housing scheme and it was run-down, ghettoised, with social issues. However, there was no hope of getting rehoused in the nearby areas. It wasn't a place I wanted to bring up my daughter. There was a lot of crime and drug misuse on the estate, with many police raids. I had to take the pram down two flights of stairs to get to street level which was problematic and alongside this, the block's main intercom system was broken for the full ten years I lived there. This resulted in homeless people sleeping in the stairwells and people taking drugs in the communal areas of the flats. Almost every day living there was stressful and it certainly wasn't ideal for myself and a child to live in a place littered with used needles, smashed bottles and stinking of urine.

By this time, Naz was around two years old and I had split up with her dad. There had been problems that couldn't be resolved and we had gone our separate ways. After trying to get help from the council I was told that the only option if I wanted to move was to relocate to another part of the country. They would pay for my transport and gave me a list of areas to visit. I felt trapped, not knowing what to do for the best. Perhaps the only future for my child was to uproot to another part of the country, where I had no family, no friends, and no familiarity. It was frightening and it made me realise that options were negligible when people have limited finances or support around them.

I was in an impossible situation and London had no answers for me. One of the options, offered to me by the council was Newcastle. Although an extremely tough decision to make, I knew I had to give it a try. Things would probably not improve in London. The repairs on the block of flats that hadn't been done for a decade were unlikely to be fixed. The council in Islington couldn't accommodate me and instead, I accepted their offer to pay for me to visit Newcastle to view a house. I had heard it was a nice city, so I travelled up with nervous optimism. The property available was a two-bedroomed house, with a front and back garden – something you could only dream about in London as a social housing tenant. It felt like paradise. Regardless of not knowing the community and it being so far from London, I knew the space and safety would provide a much more positive environment for me to raise Naz. Despite the upheaval and leaving my friends, memories, and my community, I decided I would try it. I wanted a new beginning and Walker could be that exact fresh start we needed.

A more recent photo of me and my daughter, Naz

And so it began, we moved up to the North East to begin our new lives in the community of Walker. It wasn't easy. Some neighbours and locals were lovely but there was hostility from some portions of society as well. A close-knit community can be a wonderful thing but it makes it hard for "outsiders." It was 2006 and there was the additional rhetoric around asylum seekers in the media. Perceptions amplified by the media and politics saying asylum seekers were coming to take jobs and houses, leaving British people with nothing. This was exploited and a moral panic was created in some areas, including Walker and Byker. It, therefore, made me as someone with a different skin colour, a threat and target. Before I moved in, it was perceived that I was an asylum seeker and my house was broken into. The boiler system had been sabotaged for the copper and the building stripped of anything that could be sold. There were asylum seekers in the community at the time and I was the anomaly as a British-born, black woman.

When I first moved to Walker, almost two decades ago, I wanted to use food to connect with the community. When I relocated, it was only myself and my two-year-old daughter. We were strangers, knowing nobody and far away from the home I had known for 30 years. Food brings people together in many ways and I wanted to make friends with my neighbours so I cooked my traditional dishes to share with some of them, as a gift and to introduce myself. Food is a massive part of my heritage and I've always loved cooking. I cook more Jamaican food rather than Bajan cuisine, as it is my favourite. Dishes such as ackee and saltfish, rice and peas, dumplings, jerk chicken and oxtail soup have always been on the menu in our home. The North East doesn't have a large Caribbean population and many of my neighbours had never tasted such dishes. Walker wasn't and still isn't the most diverse of communities regarding race and ethnicity, so it was important to me to bring Caribbean food and culture to them. I had entered their community but I was also a person, Naz and me, were a family who could bring kindness, friendship, and skills to their area – which was now my area. I knocked on my neighbour's doors, introducing myself, and taking along some packages of my cooking. Many neighbours were happy to try the food and very welcoming, others more reluctant. With some, a friendship grew and I still keep in touch with many, despite moving from that original street.

Rice and peas, with jerk fish – classic Caribbean food, along with homemade Jamacian dumplings, that I served to my neighbours when I moved to Walker.

Kebab Shami – an Iranian dish

Persian dish – Adas Polo

There is a local service called Building Futures East. I recently went into their building and got chatting with the staff. One of the members of the team said she could remember me and talked about when I had moved up to Walker. All those years ago, I had visited the service with some of my Caribbean foods and she had been discussing it with her colleagues. It was touching that she had remembered and appreciated the gesture. After finding out more about the service, I have since been lucky enough to join their board as a trustee.

I had never experienced racism in London, it was so multicultural. Walker was different and at times, I often (and sometimes still do) feel like an alien. I began a job in Newcastle after securing a scholarship. The scholarship involved working at Newcastle City Council four days a week whilst studying for a master's degree at Newcastle University. I worked in Human Resources, Adult and Cultural Services, and even for the then Lord Mayor (Cookson) for a time as an admin assistant. I really enjoyed my role there. Whilst I was studying, Naz attended an after-school club. I would go to work and then collect Naz, who was two and a half at the time. We would travel back home and I often felt vulnerable. On occasions, we were the target of racial abuse. I remember getting eggs thrown at us and in the winter, snowballs pelted our way. We were easy targets, new to the area and a different skin colour. I tried explaining I was British, but it didn't stop people. However, people who were not

British didn't deserve any of that hurtful, bigoted abuse either. Teenagers were horrible and at times I felt frightened, wanting to return to Islington on many occasions. But more than that, I felt heartbroken that people could be so unkind, not only to me but to other people of colour.

Things have gotten better over the years but it was an extremely distressing period. I have moved six times since I moved here to Newcastle. The majority has been because of racism but it has eased over time. It hurts my heart that I have to even think about just being accepted. I haven't broken any laws, I have the right to be here like anyone else. I've dug my heels in over the years and I'm more confident and assertive, wearing a cloak of resilience and retaliation over me. Alongside this, people have gotten to know me in the community. But none of this makes it right. Sometimes I've been pushed so far that I've reacted, my cockney accent has shocked them – thinking I would speak with a heavy African/Caribbean accent, or even possibly not understand what they were saying to me.

Society is more accepting now, of people of colour and other marginalised groups. It's been hard and it will never dissolve altogether but educating people and having zero tolerance to hate crime and discrimination is needed. My current home is in a great location. It's convenient, things are on my doorstep including transport links, amenities, and shops. I am settled, as much as I think I can be living somewhere that wasn't my birth town, but is my birth country. I've made friends with locals who are accepting and kind. It's made a difference and I'm grateful. I feel safer and content, and my children are happy here. I can get involved with activities of interest. Art, drawing, and anything creative is something I have always found therapeutic. I love to sing and have had a few, small, acting parts through a friend who is a casting agent. Naz and I have both done some acting extras work and adverts including a Gala Bingo one in 2017. This actually led to people recognising me and being less hostile, so it's been a positive and I have been known locally as the "Gala-la-la lady!"

Me and my good friend, Dave

I currently participate in a workshop locally around Universal Credit, called UC Creatives. The workshops involve following a series of research conducted by Newcastle University and York University, who interviewed people in receipt of

Universal Credits around their thoughts and experiences of the benefit. The interviews have led to a group of people who are going to express how they feel about UC through empowering art. UC Creatives want to be the voice of people who perhaps feel unheard and along with the research, help to share the impact of UC on recipients as well as challenge society's perception of people on benefits.

Some of my recent artwork

After working most of my life, I have recently been on PIP (Personal Independent Payment). I spent a few years waiting for a limited capacity award explaining that there are some jobs I would not be able to apply for and have restrictions that need to be considered regarding my health. The system doesn't work and I hope that I, the UC Creative group and also the research, can help in some way to explain this and advocate for change. I have recently secured an admin and HR role with an assisted living service for the elderly in Newcastle, which I am delighted about.

Alongside having my daughter, Naz, I have a son, Samyar (Sammy). He is seven years old and is a bright, young boy. I'm no longer with his dad but we co-parent and get on well. Sammy is half Persian, so I also cook Iranian food now, which includes dishes like Ghormeh Sabzi, which is meat cooked in green herbs and Zereshk Polo which is a chicken dish with barberries and rice. We have had problems with his education, in particular his nursery where there is a historic, ongoing issue that resulted in an injury. He is my little star and is always happy and full of life. Naz is now 19 years old and is in her last year of doing her A-Levels. She has had to change schools a few times due to bullying and my wanting to protect her. We recently talked about it and she told me that I did the best I could at the time with the tools available. It meant a lot to me, and I can see she is thriving in her education and socially. I am so blessed with my two children, who make me proud every day.

Me and my beautiful children, Naz and Sammy

Sammy and Naz

For all the challenges and at times, disgusting discrimination I have experienced, there are parts of Walker that I love. It is affordable to live here and for someone on benefits, that's critical. Some great things are going on in the community too, such as excellent local initiatives like Building Futures East, community centres like Pottery Bank and many kind people who have helped me make Walker our home, and I'm eternally grateful for that.

Evette Callender, aged 49.

Dedicated to my children, Naz and Sammy

Home From Home

In 1946, I was born in my nanna's bungalow in Merrybent, County Durham and I was christened across the road at their local Methodist church. My parents soon moved to Stanley Street in Wallsend and we lived in one of the many, privately rented terraced houses in the town. There were four of us children - I was the oldest, followed by the birth of my sisters in 1947 and 1948, and my brother in 1951.

In the 1940s we didn't have the amenities inside or out of the home that we have the luxury of in today's society. We had a tin bath and each Saturday would be bath day. The clothes horse was strategically placed around the bath, a bed sheet draped over it, to protect the bather's modesty and perhaps keep some of the heat in from the boiled water, poured into the bath that seemed to take forever to fill! There was no boiler in those days, but we knew no different. Eventually, we were able to afford a bath to be installed in the bathroom. It was bliss and made such a difference compared to the old, tin bath that had to be dragged into the lounge. It was a new development for the street and my parents allowed friends to use it. Kids had never felt so clean and it was the talk of the estate.

As a household, we weren't financially well off, but we managed and my parents saved hard. I think we were one of the first in the area to get a television and back then it was a big, old-fashioned Ferguson television. Certainly nothing like the flatscreen TVs of today, this was a bulky monstrosity but it was so beautiful to us and we were the envy of the street.

It's amazing to see how much the world has developed as time has passed. Something we now take for granted is access to a toilet. Some people have multiple toilets in their homes but when we were young we had an outside toilet. Newspaper would hang on string to be used as toilet roll and it would block the toilet. It was harsh but we didn't have any option. It used to be torture rushing to the toilet in the dark and cold, we would dash off at Olympic speeds to do our business!

Laundry washing would happen every week and we would wring the wet clothes out in the mangle before decorating the back lane washing lines with the clean washing, along with all of our neighbours drying clothes. When my mam got a twin tub washing machine with an electric mangle, it was a life changer! So many daily tasks took up a lot of time within the family – there was little convenience and families worked hard to keep on top of chores.

When I was younger we had limited toys and no technology, so we had to make our own fun and use our minds to conjure up games. Children in the local area would all play out together, the street full of youngsters having fun and not causing any harm or getting into trouble. We would play two balls and jacks. We would chase and play hide and seek. Good times and precious memories. I remember Christmas being a time of excitement for us children. Times were hard, for many families and our family wasn't exempt from this hardship. We were given an apple, orange, and bag of nuts and Mam and Dad always tried their hardest to make Christmas a celebration – and it always was.

In school holidays, Mam would take us to the beach at Tynemouth or Whitley Bay. We would travel on the train to the coast, hyper with the excitement of arriving at our destination. I remember having egg and tomato sandwiches and pop in between hours of fun with our buckets and spades, making sandcastles and splashing in the sea or in the outdoor pool at Tynemouth, which cost 9p to enter. The pool was on the edge of the sea and the sea mist would tickle our faces as we played in it. Sometimes a big wave would come over the edge and splash us but for us, it was just more fun and we were often never ready to leave and for the day to end. We would go into the Amusement Park, which was called the Spanish City at Whitley Bay. Squeals of children's delight filled the air as they played, along with places to sit, get a drink, and enjoy the atmosphere. When Mam would say it was time to go home, we would be disgruntled but grateful for a wonderful day out. During the six weeks school holidays, we would go to Darlington to stay with our auntie and cousins. Whilst there, we would take boat trips and paddle in the river. We would also visit my nanna at her bungalow, where my auntie would take gingerbread biscuits. There was always something to entertain us.

The community was tight-knit and we shopped in our local areas. The community relied on the local amenities and the shopkeepers relied on the community to keep their businesses going. My mam used to go shopping each week to the local butcher and greengrocer. There was also a local sweet shop and Mam would make sure we had a bag of sweets as our Saturday treat. We looked forward to it all week and it was always worth the wait as we tucked into liquorice all-sorts, fruit gums, or dolly mixtures. Mam used to also visit the pie and pea shop, called Broomfields or Broadbents, the fish and chip shop. Puddings were things like treacle pudding and jam roly-poly. In those days, if you wanted seconds, you had to clear your plate. Whatever was left over after Sunday dinner, would be fried up on a Monday and enjoyed. Eating was a family event, it brought us together, the stitching in the fabric of family life.

Most of my childhood was spent in Stanley Street and I attended the Bewicke School, which was demolished many years ago. I had a happy childhood. We were never spoilt but we had enough and were loved. Dad always worked, as a meter man with an electricity company and Mam worked as a secretary in a local firm as we began to get older. My dad was also a Methodist preacher and constantly wanted to help the community. Mam was very nurturing, our house was a welcoming place. Friends were forever around and felt like part of the family. That's what it was like growing up, friends in and out of each other's homes, front doors left open. Everyone knew one another, from the top of the street to the bottom. You could turn up at a neighbour's house and be welcomed in, offered warmth and food if they had it. The street had a heartbeat. A real sense of community and friendship. We've lost a lot of that these days.

Every Sunday was a day of rest. There were no shops open and there was no public transport. Instead, the community were encouraged to have a gentle day, spend time with their family, and attend church. We would frequent church at 11 am, then attend Sunday School, and return for evening prayer. Sunday was a day that we didn't even play out. Each year we would have an annual celebration at church, for the Sunday School anniversary. It was at Rosehill Methodist Church and for two-weeks, celebrations meant the church would be full to the brim of people. During the celebration, the children were asked to present pieces to the congregation that we had practised. I remember one time my sisters and me had practised our parts and it was a lovely performance. I recall the preacher commenting that the three of us siblings were beautiful sisters and asking who our parents were. I remember seeing my parents in the audience and my mam blushing! She was very proud but didn't like the limelight.

At Sunday School, we would go on trips to different, local places. One year it was Newbiggin-by-the-sea, another Crimdon Dene, and another Rothbury. We would be excited for weeks for the day trip and it was always filled with fun and laughter. The church made a great effort, including setting out tea for us with cups and saucers, alongside a bag filled with a sandwich and cake. It was a treat for all and plenty of smiles beamed from happy faces on those days. Sunday School also held Christmas parties, another highlight of the year. We would play games such as pin the tail on the donkey and musical chairs, hours of fun. Then, we would attend the pantomime through Mam's work, along with a packet of sweets and ice cream, eaten out of a tub that always seemed to taste better than in a bowl!

I tried my best at school and when I left education, I worked in an elderly care home. I really enjoyed it and the residents were lovely. I connected with them and respected them. Later in my career, I worked at the Evening Chronicle in the canteens. When I was 21 years old, I got married and moved to a property in Walkerville with my husband, Martin. My husband was over 20 years older than me and worked at Walkergate Railway Station. At the time my parents weren't happy about the age difference but eventually came round and accepted Martin. When I was 22 years old, I had my son, Stephen, who is now 54 years old. Sadly, a month after giving birth and after only being married a year and a half, I lost my husband after he suffered a fatal heart attack at only 44 years old.

It was just Stephen and me for the following four and a half years. It was hard in those days, with limited help from the government. I lost my home and moved to Walker, to McCutheon Court which was demolished during the regeneration of Walker in the early 2000s. Then I met my second husband and went on to have my daughter, Denise, who is now 52 years old and another boy, Joseph, who is aged 50. I divorced my second husband after four years. He was abusive throughout our marriage and I received support from legal aid to divorce him. It was very challenging, there were no services to support victims of domestic violence and people were not educated in the behaviours and impact of domestic abuse. The saying, "You made your bed, lie in it," was the norm and the whole idea of what goes on behind closed doors should stay private. I'm pleased there is more help for people now.

I was married a third time in 1978, to Edward. We had a child together, another daughter, Jane, who is 45 years old. Edward and me didn't get married until after we had Jane and it took him a long time to trust me. This was because I had a history with my previous husbands and also I was friendly in the area with people, including men. It was just in my nature to be sociable but elements of our relationship took time. Women's roles were different to what they are now. We had to fit into a much smaller box and society held less flexible views on women and how they should behave. There was a lot of judgement. Eventually, I gained his trust and we were very happy. Our daughter, Jane struggles with her mental health and was diagnosed with bipolar. She lives in a residential home where she receives great support and it comforts me to know that she is not alone and instead, surrounded by professionals who understand her diagnosis and can support her in the best way.

My third husband took on my other three children as his own and they all changed their surname to Dickinson when they were 18 years old. I'm also blessed to have three granddaughters. Edward was 20 years older than me and we were married for over two decades before he died in 2000. We had a lovely life together and I'm grateful I had some sustained happiness.

As for my parents, my mam passed when she was just 52 years old. She was a chain smoker and it was common in those days to be a heavy smoker. I remember Mam would forever be lighting up a cigarette, she would even take them into the bathroom. Her nicotine lipstick. No one knew the impact of smoking then and when it started to become a concern, I think half the population didn't believe it or didn't want to believe it. Dad passed around 12 years ago when he was in his 70s. At the time of his death, I didn't have a great relationship with him. After losing Mam, he struggled to cope until he met someone new. I remember Dad telling me to never give up church and I never have. My siblings are still alive and they have their own families. We don't keep in touch like we should really. Life gets in the way and everyone seems so busy. Families are strange things. We all love each other in our own ways and if we needed each other, I would hope we would all reach out.

I also have a family in the church. I am here several times a week and help out where I can. I've been a verger for around 15 years and Walker Parish Church feels like a community within itself. I support, alongside others, with opening and locking up and ensuring the place is safe. I'm here most Thursdays, Fridays, and Sundays. I also help out at weddings and funerals and do some bell-ringing, which is wonderful. The team here are lovely and it's nice for the congregation to see regular people.

I've been in my current home, in Walker, for 35 years and began coming to Walker Parish Church when I moved there. Change has been plentiful over that time; buildings gone, whole streets demolished. Housing estates have been turned to rubble, and pubs demolished. So much history is gone. Where I live, there is only one, original tenant left from the 35 years I have been there. The tenant lives next door to me and it is just us left. We say hello to our neighbours but don't really know them. Everyone is rushing around but most are very pleasant. I go to Slimming World each week and have a local friend who I help with shopping and bits and pieces. My son, Stephen pops in every week and we catch up as a family as often as we can for a meal, which is hard with everyone's commitments. I'm proud of all of my children and grandchildren. Walker is still a friendly community and people get on with one another. We can rely on each other, even if we keep ourselves to ourselves more than in the past. Places like church notice if someone is missing and they check up and ensure everyone is okay. It's important and it makes a difference.

I've completed the Christian Aid walk with the church for five years. I enjoyed them all and raised over £1,000 on one occasion from sponsors. I remember Father Phil called me the Mo Farah of

Walker! We walked from Monkwearmouth to Jarrow, along the coast, which was a lovely route for such a long walk. As I got older, it was hard to do but I thoroughly enjoyed getting involved with them when I could and planning the 26 miles, identifying toilets, having food, and chatting with all the walkers. I stopped in my 60s but it was an honour to help raise some money. Church is a home from home to me. I call it my second home. The companionship is essential to me and I hope that I also help people each week as much as it helps me.

Judith Dickinson
Verger

Judith Dickinson, aged 76

Lifeline

In 1963 I was born in Newcastle and at the age of six weeks old, I was adopted. My birth parents could not cope with another child, already having two children, a boy and a girl. I was adopted by my aunt, Jean and uncle, John, who lived in Walker. I never knew I was adopted until I was older so, Jean and John were always Mam and Dad in my eyes. My birth parents went on to have my younger brother about 18 months after I was born, so naturally, I felt even more rejected when I learnt of my true parents. Despite this, I did love my aunt and uncle, even when I found out they were my actual aunt and uncle and not who I assumed they were. Life wasn't easy, nor was it for my real siblings – even though they stayed with my birth parents, their lives were challenging. They were in and out of children's homes and there was a lot of abuse and malpractice in some of them. In many ways, I was lucky.

I have nice memories of my aunt and uncle, my adoptive parents. My uncle used to take me out and about. We didn't have lots, similar to many families in the area, but we had enough and I felt cared for. I was their only child and I enjoyed growing up in the area. My uncle died tragically when I was six years old. He was killed in Walker as he crossed a zebra crossing. What made this worse was that for years I was led to believe that he was killed by the police, with claims they had run him over. However, recently I was informed that this wasn't the case by someone who lived there at the time. It was unclear as to whether he had been hit by another car and the police turned up or if he had fallen and never recovered. This gave me an initial perception that the police were corrupt as a youngster and unfortunately, I had further negative experiences with the police as a victim of domestic abuse in the 1980s and onwards. I remember the void of his loss at the time and struggled to process my grief for many years.

After my uncle died, my aunt's health deteriorated. She had always been unwell during periods of my youth. She was diagnosed with tuberculous and cancer, amongst other ailments. When John died, she struggled and I did a lot of the tasks around the home and tried to care for her. It was really difficult as a young child and I feel much of my youth was absorbed by adult responsibilities.

You could say from a young age, I had experiences of trauma. From being rejected by my parents, which I didn't learn about until my teens, to further childhood trauma. When I was five years old, there was a catastrophic incident that happened at my cousin's house. We were all playing upstairs in one of the bedrooms - me, as the oldest, then three other cousins, each a year younger. The youngest, Alison was two. We were all playing when heard a scream. The room had a side window and the window had been opened and Alison was hanging out of it. Me and my younger cousin tried to hold her but we couldn't, we didn't have the strength and she fell to her death. I can still see her before and after she fell. As I was the oldest, in many ways I was blamed by the adults for what happened. I don't know to this day what happened, whether perhaps the latch on the window was loose or broken. I will never know but it haunts me and has all these years.

I didn't enjoy school. I was targeted and bullied and struggled to cope. I was called names for being overweight, physically assaulted, and excluded. Self-loathing multiplied and as a youngster my self-esteem was non-existent. I didn't have friends in the community as I didn't play out. After what happened to my uncle and my aunt being unwell, there was little time for socialisation and I spent a lot of time caring for her or in my bedroom. We also moved a few times in my youth, around Daisy Hill and Walker so forging friendships outside of school wasn't easy. I often felt as invisible as the air. During my youth, music was my saviour and I enjoyed playing songs in my bedroom, singing along. A little bit of escapism.

When I was around nine years old, my aunt met a new man. He moved into our home along with his mother. I didn't like either of them and his mother in particular was very cruel, tormenting me due to my weight and blaming me for eating food that I hadn't. It was another factor in making me want to leave home as soon as I could. I dreamed of flying away like a bird, away to a new place where bullies wouldn't target me.

I found out my cousins were my real siblings when I was around 14 years old. My real parents, who I thought were my aunt and uncle were always in my life but I wasn't close to them. It transpired that I was my "cousins" sibling during an argument with my real sister. It was a massive shock and my siblings had known for some time. At this point, my older brother was in the Army but my younger brother and sister were still local. I felt betrayed, rejected, and confused by the whirlwind of new information in my life that needed to be digested.

My first relationship, at the age of 15 years old, was abusive. As a young, confused, rejected girl with self-esteem that had long evaporated, I was an easy target to manipulate. He was older, at 24 years old. We were together for around four years and he became the father of my first child, my daughter. I didn't see the abuse at the time as I was flattered by this older lad being interested in me. After all the shit that had happened, I thought I was unlovable. But I know now it was a form of grooming, manipulation and misuse of power from the start. He played on my vulnerabilities and I wanted someone to love and love me after years of what felt like distress, lies, and responsibilities.

After meeting him, we moved into a flat together and I was pregnant almost as soon as I turned 16 years old. At first, he wasn't abusive but then it started, and the abuse both physical and emotional increased rapidly. The name-calling began. I was used to bullying and name calling but I had thought he loved me and I was carrying his child, so it hurt like no other name calling. Then when I was seven months pregnant, he kicked me down the concrete stairs in the block of flats we lived in. He couldn't stand that I had something growing in me that I needed to protect and all the attention I got as an expecting mother. Luckily the baby survived, despite the physical violence that he inflicted on me as if I was his worst enemy. It seemed he didn't care about me or our unborn baby. He was also cheating on me, having relationships with other women as I sat in the house most days, waiting for him to come home and hoping today was the day he changed and loved me in the right way. That day never came.

Eventually, he left me for one of the women he had been seeing behind my back. I'm not sure if I would have ever had the strength to leave him, at such a young age and with all the rejection I carried around in a metaphorical suitcase. My load was so heavy and I had such little care about myself, having been ground down to almost dust. My daughter ended up living with her father after he took me to court. I was just a kid myself and had so much mental baggage. He was a professional manipulator and made me look like I wasn't capable of being a mother. He was older, working, had a new relationship that on the surface appeared to be positive, and was financially stable so the courts went in his favour. Another massive pill of rejection I had to swallow.

I met my next partner when I was 20 years old in a local pub. We quickly got together and history repeated itself as violence began to emerge in our relationship. I fell pregnant and he assaulted me so much that I lost the baby. I didn't tell anyone the truth. Who was there to even tell? I didn't trust the police, my aunt had died when I was 17 years old, and I had no family that seemed to have ever wanted me. I was alone. As horrendous as this was, I was so emotionally damaged that I didn't have the power to leave and the promises of 'I'll change,' or being told 'It's your fault,' made me think it was all I was worth and I didn't deserve better. I began taking the contraceptive pill but fell pregnant and had my eldest son followed by two more children with him.

The abuse continued. One time he tried to drown me in the bath, another time he swung a scaffolding pole at my head whilst I was pregnant. He tried to run me over, the incidents of violence were escalating. Verbal and financial abuse was a daily occurrence, just like the sun rose, so did his anger and hatred, his misuse of control and abuse.

Days became a blur of lost hope and trying to predict my abusers' next move in a game I could never win. Food would be thrown all over the house if he didn't like the look of his dinner. Violence was common and his financial abuse meant I had to hide the odd bit of money I had. Abuse happened in so many families on the estate. It felt almost normal in my life and although my aunt and uncle weren't abusive, I knew no different in an intimate relationship.

It took me nine years to leave him. Nine years of thinking things would change or that his behaviour was my fault. That I deserved it. I was unlovable and worthless. So many times it was my children that kept me going, hoping their lives would be better than mine was but knowing somewhere that growing up in a house like they were was the beginning of the repeated cycle. Bullying, abuse, misery, and a mam who thought she deserved no better. Eyes down to the ground, never looking at the sky. My life felt dark, only my babies providing glimmers of light and hope.

I'm not sure what led me to decide after nine years that it was time to leave. Perhaps I had come so close to death that it spoke to me and warned me. I know it was thoughts of my children being without me and with that monster, that kept me alive, along with learning not to answer back. In many ways, I wasn't sure what living was – just surviving.

When I eventually left, there was little help. It was the turn of the decade, just the very early 1980s and the attitudes and awareness weren't like they are today. People lived through abuse in their marriages thinking they had to, thinking about their wedding vows. Society had the attitude of "You get on with it." and people didn't want to know what was going on around them. They minded their own business and turned a blind eye most of the time. Divorce was frowned upon and there were limited support services and understanding. The authorities weren't trained and the law reflected the lack of support and deterrents for abusers.

I did get a place with the council, in temporary accommodation but he found me. He wouldn't give up and people told him where I was, including my birth mother. I was moved again into a flat through the council, that we shared with another woman. However, she had issues with alcohol misuse and she set the flat on fire, with us all inside. Our neighbours came to rescue me and my sons and it made the local papers, but there was no acknowledgement of the bravery of the neighbours who saved us. After this I was back to square one, trying to find somewhere for us to live and keeping it secret. It seemed there was no help or safety anywhere for me and I was wary of everyone – they would only end up hurting me. I had to be strong, for myself and my sons. I returned to Walker and secured a private rented house for myself and the kids. He found me but he didn't attack me and I refused to move, knowing I would just be running away forever. Walker was my home, the very little support I had was there. I didn't want to spend my life hiding, running away to new places that felt the wrong fit. He eventually left me alone, accepting it was over and he found a new woman to manipulate. The lads never had a relationship with their father. Since leaving the father of my sons, I've never had another relationship. I know men who are decent but I never wanted to have another relationship and risk being in that position again. Instead, I tried to focus my energy on my children and building myself back up.

One of my sons lives in Manchester and the others remain local. We've had our problems, one of my sons struggled with substance misuse, but got the right help and is doing well. I have grandchildren and spend a lot of time with my eight-year-old granddaughter, who lives locally. My birth parents are now dead and I never really had a relationship with them. They had issues themselves, my mam's likely from her childhood, which was void of love. Dad drank alcohol and this became problematic as he got older. He died over 20 years ago and my birth mother died not long before the pandemic. I never got any answers or apologies.

I'm learning to make peace with things myself and realise that it wasn't my fault and that sometimes people can't or won't be the people you want them to be, no matter how hard you want it. It's just wasted energy. Relationships in families can be so fractured and history and our own experiences as children impact so much on the rest of our lives. Individuals and families are complex with so many layers, good and bad. I'm pleased I have positive relationships around me now but it's taken decades for me to build my confidence and assertiveness.

I've had some health problems and in 2014, I quit smoking and was prescribed tablets to help with this. The tablets caused constipation and six days after taking them, I was rushed to hospital and put into intensive care after my bowel burst. I was in the operating theatre for almost 12 hours whilst surgeons removed my large bowel, replacing it with a colostomy bag. I remained in the hospital for over two months and was told I was lucky to be alive. There was a lot of aftercare involved including a community nurse visiting five times a day once I was discharged home. I have hernias as a result due to complications. It was a massive impact physically and emotionally, my life changed overnight and although I was lucky to have survived the ordeal, part of me, at the time and for a long time after, wished they would have let me die on the operating table. I have tried to take my life since, but don't feel like that now. However, it took a long time to accept and deal with the emotions associated with such a life-changing illness. I also have diabetes so have to keep checking on this and monitor the impact of this on my wellbeing.

I'm 60 this year and in some ways, I'm happier than I have been throughout my life. A lot of it stems from getting involved with Pottery Bank Community Centre. I began with the well-being group once a week and found it a great place to meet people and also learn new things. I used crafts to relax and create pieces that made me and others smile. My friend brought me to the centre around two and a half years ago and I've been coming ever since. I volunteer here, helping out with the food bank, in the kitchen and with the day-to-day tasks where I can. I've seen people coming in desperate and upset and I hope I can be a small part of the help they offer. I still attend the groups; the well-being group and things like cooking, crafts, writing, and gardening. There is always something going on and always a smile, a welcoming hello and a cuppa on offer. It's a great service for the community. If I didn't have the service, I would struggle as it keeps me busy, gives me a sense of purpose and helps me so much. Mind you, they have to put up with my swearing! But it's a great place for connection and banter and I'm grateful to be part of Pottery Bank Community Centre.

Walker is my home. I'm hoping to move into a bungalow but will remain local. The community has changed over the years but some of the positives still shine through. I think the pandemic changed things and I find now, people do more for each other. I think the cost of living has also made people come together, to help each other. We are all the same, no different. We all have problems and need help and I think people realise there is no judgement in places like Pottery Bank and other services in Walker. There will always be people causing problems but there also seems to be a helping hand if you need it, you just have to ask.

Jane Hamilton, aged 59.

The Road to Community

I was born in 1974 and we lived in Walker with my grandma. She shared her home with my parents and us four kids; me, my two older brothers, and my younger sister. Dad was previously in the Army and since leaving the forces, was a long-distance lorry driver. It meant he was away quite a bit, so most of the time it was us kids, Mam, and Grandma.

Me as a baby   Dad

When Grandma passed, we stayed in the house. It was only a two-bedroomed property so all of us kids shared a room, with bunk beds crammed in. Mam had us to look after as Dad continued to work away, so life was always busy!

Me and my two brothers

My sister and me were quite close and with no other kids our age in the street, it was just the two of us playing out. I remember we used to love skipping but since it was only the pair of us, we would tie the skipping rope to a lamppost, fence, or gate and one would hold the end, flipping the rope in a skipping motion as the other jumped. We also adored our roller skates and would glide along the main street where we lived. If one of us didn't have a pair of skates - if they had been broken or no longer fit, we would share a pair, one skate each, moving along the street! Lots of fun and great exercise. We never seemed to get bored as day turned to night after hours of playing.

Mam's friend, Christine lived across the road. We were close and still are. When Christine had her daughter, Kristine, I remember my younger sister used to put her in our doll's pram and take her along the street. It was safe to do that in those days, no one bothering us and us kids just enjoying being children. I grew up with families around us, close friends who became an extension of my own family. All of us took turns looking after each other's children, then grandchildren. Friends knitted together through experience and love – always there when we needed one another.

As we got older, the four of us kids could no longer share a bedroom so we moved around the corner to a larger property, meaning the lads had their bedroom and my sister and me had ours. It was like winning the jackpot, having our own room and space. My parents are still in that house now and it's filled with generations of memories. Growing up, both of my brothers left home for work, moving to London. My younger sister and I would visit them for holidays then one of my brothers moved to Manchester and started a family. I've never moved out of the town of Walker. It's home and always will be.

Mam and Dad   Dad, my sister, and me

I attended St Vincent's Primary and St Mary's Senior School. I was the class clown, so didn't stick in, preferring to have a laugh with my peers. I was known for being a distraction and I remember with some subjects, I didn't even get the chance to step into the classroom before my desk and chair were out in the corridor. French in particular! I would end up sitting in the corridor for the full class and therefore, didn't enjoy learning. Perhaps I could have tried better to not act silly but discipline and teaching styles were different in the early 1980s. There was less help and understanding that children aren't all the same and don't learn the same way. You had to fit into a mould and if you didn't you were labelled as naughty and disruptive. However, I got through school and still have some friends I made in my education.

When I left school, my first job was in catering. It was the field Mam worked in and it was often the case that children followed the career of their parents then. I wanted the freedom and income from working and enjoyed the role.

In my early 20s, I met my partner, Kev. He's known amongst my family and friends as "My Kev" because my sister was also dating a man called Kev when I met "My Kev." We needed to distinguish between them, so the "My" was added in front. However, I knew him before we began dating as he used to be my parent's postman when I was a teenager. When I was 22 years old, I asked him out for my friend but he told me that he would rather take me out. So we went on a date and then got together. A year later, we had our first child when I was 23 years old and are still together almost 26 years later. Paige, our eldest daughter is 25 this year and Erin is 19 years old. Erin had a baby during the pandemic, which was difficult for her and the baby, but we were blessed to have Esmae arrive in the world. She was our first grandchild and Paige has since also had a baby boy, Sage, who is a year old. We are all close and Paige lives with me so it's lovely to see my grandchildren growing and developing. Another generation of memories being made.

At the time of meeting Kev, I was working in a local nursing home, cleaning. I then moved on to being a carer for the elderly. I had a career break after having Paige and I lived near to my parents so it was nice to have their support with a newborn as well as for Paige and then Erin, to grow up close to their grandparents. Many families stay in the area, the next generation securing accommodation close to their parents, sometimes even in the same street. I still live in the same street that I moved to before having my children and I'm close in location to friends, which is a lovely support. You can never feel alone in the area, there is always someone around. Good times and bad, people will cheer you on and pick you up.

Me and my grandchildren

When the children went to school I returned to work. My favourite job of all and where I worked until 2019, was as a lollypop lady with the council. It was local, just on the main road through Walker and I adored the job. The role came at the right time for me. I have experienced anxiety and depression at points in my life and when I secured the job as a lollypop lady with the council, I needed a lift, something for me and to get me out of a place that was starting to feel hopeless. Being a lollypop lady gave me a sense of purpose and the people in the community that I met every day, gave me as much as I hopefully gave them.

Kids and adults would chat and laugh with me. I got asked for advice and became a problem solver and a confidant to many. I would have so many people waving each day, smiles beaming from their faces - it was lovely. I knew all the kids' names. They would cuddle me, make me crafts, and give me gifts. The parents trusted me and would often ask me in advance to make sure their child was okay if they couldn't make the journey to school with them. I would give the kids sweets on their birthdays and felt like I knew every one of them as I watched them grow. It was so much more than a job and I was devastated when the funding ceased. The local councilor managed to keep the role going two years longer than it was meant to by securing funding, but then sadly, the funding ended altogether in 2019.

To many people, it doesn't sound much but there was something really special about the role. It felt like I got privileged access to people's lives through the relationship and trust they built with me. Almost as if that lollypop and me standing on that road, stopping the traffic so people could cross gave me a key into people's minds. It was phenomenal over the years, all the stories and dilemmas people came to me with. It became so much more than assisting people to cross the road – the road was the walkway to the mind and the problems people had. I'm still recognised, which is nice but I miss the role and I know other people in the community do. I would help out by getting newspapers for local people who had limited mobility and often I was the only person someone may chat with that day. But it also helped me and my mental well-being. I realised in my job as a lollypop lady how important it was to talk and to listen and the impact being there can make. Sometimes strangers are the people we need to talk to but strangers become friends. It was my therapy and I enjoyed the interaction. Luckily, I still see some of the kids now, although many are no longer children! But I still miss the job to this day.

I've lived in Walker all my life and the people make the community. We all know each other and it seems that when tragedy strikes, everyone comes together to support one another. Of course, there are problems, no community doesn't have issues and we have the odd rascal. But on the whole, people help. They care and they go the extra mile for their neighbours, their friends, and family. When people come together and support, it's amazing what the outcome is. When anyone needs to know what's going on, the community finds out – usually, I'm one of the people asked!

Walker has changed over the years, good and bad. It's home to my memories, my past, and my future is here. Unfortunately, crime is an issue, like it is everywhere, and young people are vulnerable to gangs or being victims of crime. There used to be a safety in the community that doesn't seem to exist anymore. No more leaving the front doors open. Now we are all in the house by 9 pm and the front door is locked. It's sad in many ways. However, I do know that there is always help if anyone needs it – there is always someone close who would help out, no matter what. That's community and I don't think that will ever die.

Me and my friend, Christine

Me and my friend, Kristine

I come to Pottery Bank Community Centre as much as I can, with my friends Christine and Kristine. It's a welcoming place and there is always someone to chat with and plenty of activities going on. It's an asset to the community and for me, it's been nice to try new activities but also get me out of the house. My friends have been there through the good and the bad and are a medicine I could never get from a doctor. I'm very grateful and along with my family, I have the most amazing people around me who keep me well.

Linda Parkinson, aged 48.

Dedicated to my family and loved ones.

Stepping Away from the Darkness

I struggle to remember much of my childhood. It's blanked out in many ways through illnesses and trauma, only told through piles of photo albums. I was born in 1971 into a body that brought with it an assumption that I would be male. The sibling to an older brother, we lived with my parents in Crawley, West Sussex.

From an early age I knew I could not live as the person I experienced myself to be, who I should have been born as. And for a massive part of my life, I felt I could never be myself, both gender-wise and with the way my brain worked. Of course, this had to be buried and forgotten. Neither of these things were understood or supported in the 1970s. Only within the past few years, and after postponing seeking diagnosis for another decade, I have been diagnosed with autism. When I was a child, I could never have been diagnosed as autistic. This, along with poor mental health, identity confusion, and gender expectations, made for a difficult childhood and adolescence where I never felt the right fit.

School taught us to conform, to "fit in." That being very intelligent wasn't really a good thing and that I shouldn't "shine." Instead, just be like everyone else and get on with it – photocopied humans. From a young age, I knew I didn't "fit in" and tried to find my place and acceptance for many years. When I was eight years old I was able to complete maths work aimed at 13-year-olds. I remember my teacher at the time, who was wonderful, going home each night to try and find work aimed at older students to keep me occupied and advance my skills. Of course, it was very different to what the rest of the class was being taught and therefore more work for her as a teacher. But she would return, with different questions for me to explore the answers to. She was almost the only teacher who encouraged me.

Culture in schools in the 1970s offered little deviation from the teaching methods for any children who presented as different or learnt differently, at both ends of the scale. I remember a girl in my school who was told she was "stupid," and "thick" as she couldn't grasp maths in the way most students could. It's clear now she had a different way of learning. It didn't make her stupid, it just meant she absorbed, reflected, and learnt another way. That girl became an adult and taught herself maths before writing a book teaching maths teachers how to teach students who needed to learn in different ways. Things are better in education now. There are still problems but more understanding and empathy on the whole. Outside of school, my parents did try to nurture my mind. We looked at the Society of Gifted Children and a scholarship for private school but things weren't pushed, so nothing came of it.

Me as a child

I was a bit of a loner in and out of school. However, I did have one friend – a boy who was also a lost and lonely soul, who was intelligent and targeted as a nerd. It was nice to have companionship with a friend who I felt I could relate to, in some ways. Of course in others, we were polar opposites. I enjoyed puzzles, games, and books when I was younger and I still love puzzles, in particular Sudoku. As a youngster, I would do things like working out the square root of three to thirty decimal places! Through the early 1980s, I became somewhat of a child entrepreneur through buying and selling second-hand books. I was selling around 200 books per week and would attend book fairs, and market stalls, and sell to second-hand book shops. I would read a book a day and as a child, I loved all the classical sci-fi such as Heinlein, E.E "Doc" Smith, and Asimov. I also enjoyed the Fighting Fantasy books that were so much fun – starting with The Warlock of Firetop Mountain.

As a teenager life became more of a struggle. I would hide away a lot, and the innocence and carefree feelings of childhood dissolved. Not that I ever felt, even as a young child that I was carefree. My mind never really let me. I continued to try and enjoy hobbies and interests. When I was 10 years old, the ZX81 computer was released and at 12, the Spectrum computer arrived! I remember typing in what felt like 15,000 lines of machine code to play a computer game that wasn't very good! School became increasingly challenging as a grew up. I found it dull and none of it seemed relevant to life. I became more depressed as a teenager and first remember feeling depression as a thing when I was 12 years old. My mum told me there were many indicators before this time, but I cannot remember them and she wouldn't tell me anything about them. However, when I was 12 years old I stopped being able to function at school and around people. I was taken out of normal lessons and placed in the "Unit for Maladjusted Children." It continued and at 13 years old I saw a psychologist for the first time who wrongly diagnosed me with schizophrenia with no follow-up whatsoever.

I remember there being a writer in residence at school and I began writing as a form of coping and expression. It was a challenge to manage, I had so much going on in my head that it felt like a mind race with no finish line. I remember getting an A+ for a suicide letter we had to write as part of an English topic. Life felt like I was going through the motions and the exciting time of teenage years that were promised through the media, never materialised. In many ways, it was survival with the constant, overbearing shadow next to me that I just didn't fit in.

At the age of 15 years old, I saw my first psychiatrist. It was awful and the small part of the trapped 15 years old in me, still despises her. I didn't say a word during the session and was almost watching the session from above, recalling everything in that room. A week later we returned for a family session and I was told I needed medication, ECT and long-term hospital care, in another town, away from home. Luckily, this didn't happen. I think it would have killed me and looking up that particular hospital recently, the only information I could find was a survivors group which discussed sexual abuse that occurred on the premises. It was a lucky escape. I was distraught the following days and my parents looked into alternative therapies.

I attended a college and therapy centre in Kent that was saturated in new age, alternative support for mental well-being. At the time, it was of interest to me and the whole set-up and model of support felt much more holistic. My parents were willing to explore all options to help me and I was grateful for that. At White Lodge, I received counselling and attended courses. They were good people and I truly feel the experience saved my life. Looking back and as a parent myself now, it must have been frightening and distressing for my parents. They would have seen something very different in me than what I perceived of myself. My whole childhood as a person who didn't feel complete, who was faded as if an eraser had blurred my edges. An unhappy, confused child. When I began attending White Lodge, it was as if my parents knew that I would eventually die if I didn't get some support that suited me as an individual. It was probably the best thing Mum ever did for me.

Dad was always supportive but didn't say much. He was from that generation of silenced emotions in males, being born nine months after the start of the second world war. His father didn't return until after the war ended and during that time his father was captured in Italy, escaped and fought with rebels in the mountains. I feel that perhaps he was autistic himself, but obviously, he was never diagnosed as so many weren't until the last few decades.

Two months after seeing the first psychiatrist and after engaging with the college in Kent, I did the exam for my maths O-Level a year early and obtained a grade A. At 16 years old, I began A-Levels then thought I was expected to attend university. I had wanted to study psychology, especially after my own experiences. However, when I was studying my A-Levels, in a small period of stability, I began to try and find myself – or at least a version of myself I could function with and perhaps even enjoy life with. It included starting a relationship that lasted around five years. I found A-Levels boring and I was studying science subjects when I wish I would have chosen others in retrospect. I would have loved to have studied music. However, I continued my education and attended Bradford University and studied bio-medical sciences for a term. I didn't enjoy it and it made me feel depressed and pressurised with expectations. One night, soon into my studying I remember going out searching for some help and looking for the Samaritans. I went down the wrong street and ended up in the red-light district of Bradford. I recall a sex worker coming up to me, a naive young man, asking if I wanted 'business' when all I wanted was to find the Samaritans! Then the riot police landed, on the search for drugs and criminals. It was a night to remember but not for finding the help I needed.

I transferred courses and began studying interdisciplinary human studies. This included literature, philosophy, psychology, and sociology.

However, I didn't stick with this either because I believed I was being called to a different life, studying another subject in a different town. I completed an academic year but the internal struggle of my identity and inability to manage my mental health kept creeping up on me like the most painful and persistent of heartburn. I was vulnerable and confused and then something else came into my life, God. It was all the wrong Christian influences but I was looking for something in my life that I had never been able to obtain – an understanding of how to manage my feelings and an insight into how to navigate life. It had always felt like a bad fit for me, like the shoes that were too small and pinched with every step. Pain, confusion, inability to process thoughts and lack of understanding around myself led me to being identified and influenced by people who I thought at the time could help but who had their own rigid, dangerous ideologies and agenda.

I felt worthless and thought my life was pointless so they offered a solution, my "salvation." I vulnerably entered into a religious group that made me feel religion would cure me of all the "badness" in me. That the religious role models knew best and would help me get on the right path of health, happiness, and "normality." At times this resulted in praying up to six hours a day. Church became an obsession and I thought that if I prayed properly, God might make me happy. One time in Bradford it was around 3 am and I was walking with a friend down the main road in the city. The police stopped us, asking where we were going and what we were doing. Our answer and the truth was that we were heading to the cemetery for a prayer meeting and had just left another prayer meeting. The group at the church had recruited many young people, all with a level of vulnerability. It became my whole existence and meant I dropped out of other things that were in my life that were healthy and supportive, such as a hiking group that used to meet every Sunday.

I ended up leaving Bradford about a year later and moved to Aberystwyth to study theology, which was where I met Beth, who would become my wife. I made this move because I hallucinated the voice of God telling me to, while half asleep on the train. I didn't have the knowledge to understand hypnagogic hallucinations so to me it had to be God rather than just a thing brains do sometimes that's not even a mental health issue. Similarly when I got visited by the "old hag" as they'd say in Canada, I had no understanding of sleep paralysis.

Whilst living in Aberystwyth, I visited the Jesus Army after having been invited by a close friend and subsequently became a member in my early 20s. I was taken there by a friend as the Jesus Army had a strong image of "Biblical manhood." I wasn't manly enough and believed I had to be. Religion had taught me that. Society had taught me that. I was taken to the Jesus Army to teach me how to be a proper man. It was initially a Baptist church in Northamptonshire, evangelical but relatively normal. In the late 1960s, hippy revivals got into Christian communities and the Jesus Army expanded by buying buildings for members to live in, having different levels of membership and a covenant vow. The covenant vow included a life-long commitment to their church rather than following Jesus anywhere in your life. They focused on heavy discipling and shepherding for a while, which caused a lot of problems. Many homeless people were recruited, or people who had addiction issues, or mental health issues. Susceptible people looking for a way out of their current life, an escapism, or an answer and acceptance.

I joined in the 1990s and in recent years many historical abuse claims came to light covering decades. There was a great deal of psychological abuse and young people growing up in the church and both men and women there were physically and sexually abused by church elders, parents and other church members and visitors to community houses. There was a legal report a few years ago that was published. It is hundreds of pages long and details some of the abuse. The Jesus Army is sometimes called a religious cult and in my opinion, it was due to the preaching which was limiting and abusive. It was another institution, somewhere else to instil in me the ideology that I couldn't be who I wanted to be and had to focus on being a man, a manly man at that! The Jesus Army segregated genders; brothers and sisters. On my first evening there, I refused to sit with the brothers at mealtimes. I did make some friends there, three people in particular who I was close to and who are all now dead through drug misuse. We all saw things, heard things, and were victims ourselves of terrible things that happened there. I hadn't got as deep into the Jesus Army as I could have and as others had – especially those who lived in their accommodation. I entered engaged to Beth. If I had arrived single, the Jesus Army pressured people to take a life-long vow of celibacy. I also didn't take their covenant vow as it didn't feel right following the Jesus Army and not just Jesus. They would tell people that God hates them if they left. I got depressed again, took the chance that God may hate me and left the Jesus Army. I looked around for other churches but we left Northampton before I fully settled anywhere. And when I knew we were leaving I went back to the Jesus Army because of friendships and the better quality of free food!

Beth and I married when I was 25 years old in Aberystwyth. After a short stretch in Crawley and a job in Korea going wrong, we moved to Northampton because it was Jesus Army land and much cheaper than Crawley. However, we then moved again, this time to Lancashire. She was and always has been supportive of my mental health. All the religion, medication, the expert mental health people who didn't give me expert advice, Beth made it all possible to survive. She was the person who helped me through, supporting me in a way nothing and no one else had. My scaffolding, holding me up. I was never cured when we were married. I never recovered from my illness like you may a cold. But I was able to manage it better most of the time. I had support from her and that was the best medicine I could have asked for. She was amazing and still is. She stood by me, my crutch when I needed it, my strength when I felt weaker than a newborn kitten, my power when I felt vulnerable. She was always there, caring and loving me. For almost every year of our marriage, I know she wondered if I would survive that year, yet she never left. A constant in a world that felt so fragile for me. She put up with my brain, my weirdness, and 20 years of strong religiously motivated self-hatred and homophobia. We had our son, Kit, in Lancashire. He is now 22 years old and we are both so proud of him for the person he is and his achievements.

Our wedding day

We remained in Lancashire for three years, where I was a Baptist lay preacher but life continued to be a struggle. I was headed towards another breakdown, self-harming before my sermons. Psychiatric drugs never made me well. They failed to helped alleviate experiences of mental distress. I also hadn't accessed substantial counselling. Then we moved to North Wales - a beautiful place where we lived for ten years. I had periods of managing but the ghosts inside kept haunting me. Feelings of despair and pointlessness remained. I had the heavy darkness that was always there, even on the best days, constantly clawing away on the inside. Never going away. Never letting up. I would look at religion believing I had to pray more, try more, and perhaps the darkness would go away. But it didn't help. God never took it away.

I'd always had unhealthy and unhelpful Christian influences which feels a shame. Had I been studying in Bradford 15 years later, I could have attended the Anglican chaplaincy called Desmond Tutu House where Chris Howson was the chaplain, who now works in the North East and is phenomenal.

Despite this, Beth kept me alive. At this point, my gender identity had been buried so deep within myself that it was trapped in a cell that I couldn't even access. A silent scream that I dismissed as I tried to go about life. It had been drilled into me that it was shameful and those desires and feelings made me a monster. I couldn't address it so couldn't share my emotions about feeling I was in the wrong body with Beth, even though she was the most supportive person in my whole world. Of course, now I know I was never in the wrong body. I am in my body, the only one I have and it's only the expectations and impositions of society that cause transgender people to believe anything is wrong. Or worse, that they should only expect to be accepted socially and legally if they endure major surgery while they're simultaneously abused and insulted both for having surgery and for deciding not to. People, papers, and politicians can say such vile things about people like me who only want to get on with our lives in peace. It's truly frightening to exist right now.

It happens to cisgender people too in other ways causing so many wonderful people to become miserable about their bodies. Too thin, fat, tall, short, freckled, pale, dark, bald, hairy, asymmetrical, there's always something wrong they're told. Something to lead to self-harm, to eating disorders, self-hatred, addictions, sometimes death. There is something fundamentally wrong with our image-selling society that leads people to hate themselves for their faces and their bodies.

We need to change society. Flee the airbrushing and filters. Learn that we are already okay. We need to love and accept each other in our magnificently human physical variety. We may sometimes change our bodies to make our lives easier, as I do with hormones just like many women do and may be forced to do with surgery if I want freedom. But our bodies are our bodies and deserve to be loved not abused. None of us, none of us are in the wrong body.

Life continued, a cycle of struggles then we moved to Newcastle in 2011, eight days after my 40th birthday. Life began at 40 in a crumbling bungalow! We had left Wales because our estate became very student heavy and the new home we had plans to move to, all went off plan as Beth was made redundant. Beth suggested moving to Newcastle as she had friends there, so that's what we did. My first impressions were that it was cold – it was a bad winter! Newcastle was a big city compared to Bangor where we had left. A priority was needing to find a church as I was a very enthusiastic Catholic when we moved. One nearby wasn't friendly and the other wasn't religious enough for me and the desperate brainwashing that lingered within me.

Me in 2011   Me in 2012

I remember soon after arriving in Newcastle that there was an artist collective pop-up shop on Grainger Street. Here, I saw a poster for shape note singing, which I had done in Lancashire. It made me feel that perhaps I could be at home here. Then I began to settle in and found the community friendly and options of activities in the area. I got involved with the Philosophy Society for a couple of years. The community felt more creative, diverse, and welcoming.

I left the Catholic church and joined an Anglican church. Strands of darkness started to loosen, glimmers of light pushing through and I began to look at myself differently. Eventually, in 2013, it all fell down – the wall, the locked door, the buried feelings of identity. Pentecost sparked it and I remember that we had to dress in red for the tradition. It was just me and the visiting preacher. I was leading much of the service that day, at least the first half. Instead of just dressing in red, I wore nail varnish, called Decadence. Soon after I sent a very long email to Beth and in it, I asked if it would be okay for me to get myself a gothic-style "man's" skirt. The next morning, she gave me one of hers. Things then began to change quite quickly. On 4th June 2013, I stood in front of a mirror, dressed as myself. That was the first time I called myself Clare. My name came through a dream! I always say that most people are named by their parents, mine came to me prophetically. Beth completely accepted me. She was one of the easier people to tell. I had total support at home which made things a lot more manageable. Her opinion and her acceptance were crucial. I needed that and I received it. Kit was also so accepting and it meant more than I will ever be able to express. It was my life lottery ticket and I could share it with the people most important to me.

Becoming Clare

Everything from that day began to fall into place and in 2015 I was finally diagnosed with autism. I remember a theology student I met in the 1990s, who I later saw again at an autism conference. Her father was autistic and when I met her again, she was head of a special needs school that she'd completely transformed from something quite abusive and failing into something excellent with the help of an autistic woman, Dr. Yo Dunn who I also met a few times. She told me she had suspicions in the 90s that I was autistic. However, even if I would have been diagnosed at that time (which was extremely rare), I wouldn't have believed her. The only images of people with autism in those days was a person or child completely shut in within themselves or Rain Man. In around 2000, Mum had heard about Asperger's on the radio and told me she thought that I had it. I didn't think so. Years later, I remember taking Simon Baron-Cohen's autistic quotient test and scoring 42 or 43 out of 50. I recall taking it again when I came out as transgender, as I was so much happier and I still scored the same.

After my diagnosis, I accessed some pockets of community support. There wasn't a great deal in the area but I did receive support from the church I had joined as Clare, the Metropolitan Community Church, which was originally started by Christians to be Christian without being condemned for being gay. At the time I joined, there were also a lot of members who were autistic so that really helped me. I left the church seven years ago, I gave it up for Lent! I didn't leave on bad terms, it just wasn't for me anymore. Like an old jumper I was no longer fond of or just didn't really want or need. I still communicate with many of the people I met there. It served a purpose and more of a purpose than any other religious establishment had in my life in many ways as it allowed me to be me and accepted me as Clare.

Being myself and being accepted sort of meant I didn't need religion anymore. I didn't have to hide myself, pray that I could live in a gender I wasn't and kept my true identity locked away, shackled with guilt, disgust, and fear. It was out and I could be me at last. Religion became redundant and I began seeing all the unhealthy sides of religion and what it did to me. I remember early on in my time at the Metropolitan Community Church when an ex-member told the pastor at the time that it had been a safe place to lose her faith. The pastor had replied that it was a great thing. She was a good pastor and a good person. I marched at Pride with them last year, a great bunch of people. Pride is a good word, despite being told in church that it isn't and it is one of the deadly sins. That you be humble, not proud. But in the movement, it is about a voice, the opposite of humiliation.

Despite living as Clare, my mental health deteriorated again. I ended up seeing a psychologist for the first time receiving more than two sessions. However, often when psychology begins to understand you, the NHS budget expires. I had so much to deal with that had been oppressed for so long and was now visible to me and the world. I received a diagnosis of dissociative identity disorder (DID). Sometimes I feel this is right and I think should be otherwise specified dissociative disorder (OSDD). It depends on how I am and how stressed I feel. I almost received a PTSD diagnosis and a panic disorder diagnosis. I have had 18 diagnoses given to me over the years and feel around 1.8 perhaps fit me! We can all be found in the diagnostic book somewhere. But we are all individuals. Labels, diagnosis, conditions. Sometimes it's just about being seen as a person and not receiving questionnaires every week to see how we feel about ourselves and our lives, which can actually make us feel a lot worse.

As a trans woman and as someone who at last can be who I want to be, I would prefer never to talk about trans issues again. However, every day I see something in the media that makes me know we have to keep talking about it. Hate, transphobia, abuse and attacks against the trans community. Recently, a 16-year-old trans-girl got murdered. There are rallies against trans people and one locally that quoted Mein Kampf to support their views. Hate crime is a big issue for marginalised groups, including trans people. The internet has made life so much better with some elements yet so much worse with others. Like many transgender people in the UK, I am afraid of what may be coming. The language from government and media is getting harsher and laws are being proposed in Parliament that would make it harder to live openly and freely as who we are. We are just us, all of us, individuals. Life would be much simpler if we were all just allowed to be ourselves (and not harm ourselves or others) and everyone just let us get on with it.

When I came out in 2013, my dad had frontal lobe dementia so was struggling with his health. My mum had this to cope with but also had her own health problems, having experienced and survived cancer. However, I was planning on going to visit her with Kit and I wanted to be me. I told her about my identity and she went away for 24 hours, researched transgender then came back and accepted me. More people accepted me than I thought would, but there was still that rejection. It was nothing compared to the struggles I had endured during my life and I was just happy to be myself at last.

Mum became ill pretty quickly after that with cancer number four. She died in August 2014 and by this time, Dad was in a care home. I'm grateful for the time with my mum where I could be myself. After years of my parents having to see me struggle and struggle themselves as helpless parents, restricted by a system that didn't work, fit, or care, there was a level of peace. There was acceptance and happiness that I had at last and that Mum could witness. My parents came to Newcastle when I was living as myself, so they got to see me in my community, content. It was important and I'm grateful. My brother also accepts me as Clare. He lives in another part of the country so we don't see each other much but acceptance is key.

I'm still married to Beth and we have a marriage certificate with our correct names on it, which is important. We are still in a relationship but we do not live together. Instead, we live a few miles apart, which keeps us connected but is easier for both our difficult heads and sensory needs.

Byker has a reputation but it's a good place. There are social problems, like in so many places, but there is a lot of good. It's a close-knit community with good people, resources, and diversity. Each night I look out of my window to all the lights of the city and it's magical – I never take it for granted. I get out and about as much as I can. I love nature, I feel at peace with the nature around the area. Rivers, parks, the coast and countryside in the North East. It's stunning, but I also see beauty in the simplest of things. The first pop of colour from the flowers in spring, the park bench that holds so many stories, the street art that tells a tale. I'm lucky that I live here and I'm in a place where I can absorb nature, the community, and life. I can appreciate things around me, instead of existing in a fog of unhappiness, anxiety, and a world that was grey. Contentment is a precious thing, when you don't have it, life is painful. I have other problems, as we all do. My health is poor and some days things are a real struggle. But contentment with myself is a great healer. I hold so much less hate for myself. I accept myself as a queer, autistic weirdo and I am fine with that. Things come back, I will always have stuff to work through and that's okay.

Me – out and about in my local area

I use writing as a tool for my well-being and I enjoy creating poetry. Six years ago I performed some of my work in public for the first time and I have continued to write and share at opportunities. I write about things in my head, experiences I have had, and observations. Hopefully, people can relate to it. I also play guitar and love music. I've been in choirs, including a local choir, called She Choir. My health and the pandemic changed my ability to get involved with certain things locally, but hopefully, I can get back to activities I enjoy in the future. I love Sudoku and have beaten the world champion online at times. I'm not as quick now I'm older but I still enjoy it.

At Pride

My mental health is okay, even despite the pandemic and my physical health deteriorating. I was diagnosed with fibromyalgia earlier this year and some days I struggle. But I keep walking and try to be aware of and accept my limits. I need to learn to commit to what I must do in order to make life as good as possible. To unlearn habits and rules I have had to conform to all my life and re-write my own rulebook in a way that doesn't result in punishment if I can't do it.

Life is difficult but life is also a wonderful gift. I have passed the age of 50 and never expected to achieve that. Every day is a new and unexpected treasure but just as you have to dig through grey rocks and mud to find jewels, life cannot always have the immediate sparkle of diamonds. Neither can our amazingly complicated minds in our squidgy, little, incredible brains. Even the grey rocks are gifts and although sometimes I can be a massive grump, I give thanks daily because I am still alive and accept and lovingly embrace the complexities of being who and what I am. In that self-embrace, I can learn better to accept the thousand facets in your diamond soul too.

To quote one of my favourite musicians, Ren;

I must not forget, we must not forget that we are human beings – Hi Ren by Ren.

Clare Matthews

Our Granny, Our Queen

I was born in Walker in the mid-1980s, grew up here, and still live here with my partner and two children. My family moved into different houses as I grew up, with some of our former properties being demolished as part of regeneration. Places filled with memories bulldozed down and new houses built or areas left as grassland, holding times gone by in the earth. We moved into different streets, but always within Walker, near to our extended family. We lived next to my auntie and when she moved, we often followed. Always close by.

I have an older brother and a younger sister. As adults, we all lived in Walker but now my brother lives in Whitley Bay, not too far away. I have a large family on my dad's side but we don't get the chance to see them much. On my mam's side, there is a massive family, many of which live close by. Mam was one of eight siblings and when I was growing up, big families were still the norm in Walker. Everyone knew each other and would look out for one another. These are some of the old traditions of Walker. Families surrounded one another and neighbours were family; blood or otherwise.

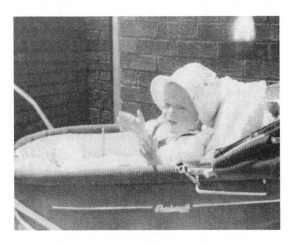

Me as a baby

My friends also came from large families and many of my friend's grandmothers were "Walker Nanna's," who were perhaps more modern in lots of ways and swore like troopers! My granny was a traditional, cuddly, old-fashioned Granny, like the perfect, cartoon depiction. I called her "our Queen," and that's exactly what she was – precious, important, and the head of our family. Childhood was about family, adventure, and fun and this included Granny. We would spend summers at her house or holidaying in the caravan. I first went abroad when I was ten years old, but alongside that, we spent the summers in the streets, playing games and popping in to see Granny. A precious childhood that I would never change. We would have homemade chips from someone's house, wrapped in newspaper and dished out to all the kids as they played in the streets. Smiles, shouting, laughing, and entertaining ourselves. We would play curbs, hide and seek, and "knocky-nine doors." It was a great time and kids could be real kids, away from social media and mobile phones. The neighbours looked after each other and each other's kids, it was a real community and felt safe.

I still have friends from my youth that I remain close to. Some childhood friends were a little older than me and as we grew up, many of them would drink alcohol. I was "the bairn," the youngest girl and the tag-along. There were only a few years between us all, but when you are younger, it seems to be endless years separating you as you try to fit in. Luckily, I was always accepted and we remain close today.

Granny, me, and my cousin, Sean

Granny and me

I loved primary school and enjoyed the first two years of high school but after that, it wasn't much fun. We used to abscond, or "wag-it," as we called it. I would go to school, get a tick on the register, and then leave the premises! I just wanted to do my own thing, as many teenagers did and still do. Thinking we were cool, we would all leave school and have a day of hanging about the streets and parks. I never thought about it until I left school, but if the fire bell would have went, I would have been in big trouble and perhaps put others a risk, given my tick of attendance was there but I was nowhere to be seen! I got away with wagging it for ages. I used to take my younger cousin to school, before getting my tick and leaving. Then one time, my cousin told my parents and my secret was uncovered. One night I came in from school and my mam asked if I'd had a good day, knowing I hadn't been in. I had been rumbled! I left school at 16 years old, having completed no exams. I had been in top sets at school, with a lot of potential but I just couldn't go through with doing my exams. I wasn't sure what it was, whether it was anxiety or confidence, but it was a barrier I just couldn't get over.

After school, I got involved with training through an organisation called Rathbone. I had a passion for design and in particular, designing clothes. Rathbone signed me up to do design at college and I attended an interview. On the day I was due to start college, I got halfway there and just couldn't go in. That barrier was back and once again, it defeated me. I'm an anxious person and can see how anxiety and my fears have held me back in the past and still to this day.

When I left training I began a job cleaning caravans in Berwick. We used to get collected in a minibus and then dropped back off at the end of the day. I had this job for a few holiday seasons and enjoyed it before progressing to cleaning in hotels. I secured a job at The Newgate Hotel, which used to be in Newcastle and then moved on to The Jury's Inn. It was hard work, we had to clean a lot of rooms in an allocated time frame, but it was a good job.

I met my partner, Olly, when I was in my late 20s. We got talking in 2012, on an internet dating site. He's from Manchester but was working in Wales when we first connected online. Within two weeks we were smitten and I got his name tattooed on my body! By week four, he left his life in Wales and moved up here, to Walker. At the time, I lived with my dad and hadn't even met Olly in real life. But we just knew we wanted to be together. I told Dad that Olly was just coming up to visit, but he never left. It was surreal meeting him for the first time at the train station in Newcastle. I was so nervous to see him in the flesh for the first time but it was amazing. We laugh about it now as he got off the train at the cold station in Newcastle and was dressed all in white. Head to toe in white clothes and I just thought that I can't keep clothes white for all my trying! But we were still the perfect match, even if his clothes would suffer. When we met in real life, it felt like I had always known him. Olly got on with my family straight away, as if it were meant to be. He had uprooted to a new place, a new community, and had to adapt to a new family of strangers. But he settled well and I knew he was the one for me.

Olly quickly became part of the family and we soon went on to have our own family. Just before this time, I was promoted to supervisor at work. I also went to another branch of the hotel to be an accommodation manager for a short period. It was during this role, that I found out I was pregnant. I returned to the company once my daughter was born, taking on the role of linen porter, which I loved. I worked for the organisation for eight years, it was a great place to work and my colleagues were lovely.

We are lucky enough to have two, beautiful children. Elvis is our ten-year-old son and Aaliyah, our daughter, is eight years old. She gets called Doris because people can't pronounce her name! They are both brilliant kids and I'm so proud of them. We are like other couples and we've had our struggles, especially after we had our second child. It was hard with two young children and we had a period where we split up briefly, after a massive bust-up. We worked through the difficulties, we loved one another and had two, precious children, who needed both their parents. It was make or break and as I let Olly return home, we worked on our relationship and became stronger than ever. It's hard, life can be difficult, managing demands as a woman, and trying to be the best parent and partner you can be. Relationships need to be equal, fair, supportive and trusting. We are now stronger than ever. Love was the glue that kept our family together and we will stay stuck together, even through the most challenging of times.

Me and my family, Salou (2018)

I eventually left working in the hotel industry after a role came up at Pottery Bank Community Centre for a domestic. It was on my doorstep and somewhere I had been a regular attendee at as a child. I began using Pottery Bank Community Centre over 20 years ago. First, it was with the Kid's Café scheme, that my mam was part of. It focused on cooking, eating together, and nutrition. I then began volunteering here. My kids have also been part of the community centre, so it feels like it is part of our family in many ways. I can see the changes in the community centre over the years as well as the changes in the wider community. Pottery Bank Community Centre is a home-from-home for us, both mine and my children's childhoods have involved the centre. My sister used to be the receptionist here, so we have all had close links to it and I hope future generations continue to benefit from it as we all have. When I started at Pottery Bank we had a lot of women's courses, including health and social care, gardening, sewing, and cooking. My mam manages Catering Company, based here. I'm not a cook myself, but my partner is a chef, so I leave the skill of cooking for us all to him! Things have changed over the years including resources and the community using the service. But there is a cohort of people who have used Pottery Bank Community Centre for years, myself being one of those people. Even during the pandemic, they offered support, and I hope they continue to thrive.

As things changed around during my childhood, adolescence, and adulthood, there were always consistencies in certain places and people. Things that sometimes you think will be around forever, never to change, never to die. Like my granny, or Mrs. Cox as she was known in Walker. In a way, it felt like Granny was invincible, even as I saw her ageing over the years and slowly disappearing. I lost my granny in December 2022, after she just turned 94 years old. She had been such a monumental part of all of our lives. I was lucky enough to have her for over 35 years, she's helped shape me to be the woman I am today, alongside my mam and other strong women in my life.

Granny was the centre of our family and we all helped care for her towards the end of her life. She had always lived locally and after she had my mam, Granny moved into a house on Merton Road, Walker, where she remained for 60 years. We called her house Paddywell House as there was a well in her garden and Granny used to call all of her dogs over the years Paddy! Every single dog! Whilst houses were demolished around her, streets regenerated, and people came and went, Granny was there in her home. In the end, we had to move her out as her health was deteriorating and her house became infested with rats. It was a large, four-bedroomed family home and even though for the short period before her death, Granny didn't live there, it will always be her home. She lived in a local complex called Treetops for the last few years of her life. I struggle to walk past her home on Merton Road now. It's bittersweet; filled with such memories of love but imprinted with the pain of loss.

There was a tree in the garden of Granny's house that I had never seen until after she had moved. I compared two photos we had, from when we were younger to when she left the house. A tree stands, tall and proud in her garden. It had been planted when we were younger and it grew as we grew but I always thought it was there, towering over the garden. But we were too busy having fun to realise. I'm pleased it will continue to grow, in our "Queen's" front garden.

The tree at Merton Road, that grew as we grew up

Granny's door was always open and welcoming. The fire was constantly on and there was always food on the go. Her cupboards were like a shop, even in her later life, as if she still had to feed her eight children that now had children and grandchildren of their own. But there was something special, something precious about Granny's. I could turn up, anytime and be welcomed in. After a hard day, I could go and sit with Granny, in the cosy warmth and not say a word. It was a place of acceptance, rest, reflection, and reassurance. A place and a person like no other. Granny had a diagnosis of dementia and a care package in place. However, it was inadequate and she wasn't drinking and eating properly. This led to her being hospitalised in October 2022. My aunt fought to get her home but could not get the appropriate care package. My aunt decided we could try to cover her care as a family and planned to bring her home. Sadly, Granny passed away the day before we were due to bring her home. She was a strong, determined, no-nonsense woman and we knew she would do things the way she wanted, including when she passed.

She was such a loving grandmother, the way a granny should be. A proper, traditional granny, whereas grandmothers these days aren't the way they were years ago. They still love and have those personal qualities but they look less like the grannies of my childhood. Granny was like a little farmer's wife with her skirt and pinny and socks pulled up. I have so many precious memories and so do my children, which is important. The night before the funeral, my auntie and I spent the night laughing at memories of things Granny had done and said, and times spent with her. It was what she would have wanted, us laughing at the good times. But she is such a loss. She had 23 grandchildren and over 40 great-grandchildren. My children came to the funeral and my son, Elvis wanted to walk with the funeral director up her street. I was so proud of them that day and I'm pleased they have their memories of Great Granny.

Granny's 88th birthday   Granny and Aaliyah

I could fill a book with memories of my granny, she really was and always will be my Queen. Out of all the things I'll remember about her, one thing that has been and will always be passed from generation to generation is singing lullabies. From as far back as I can remember, she always sang to us and to every baby she ever held. Even now, if I sit back and close my eyes I can still hear her voice and feel her tapping her hand gently on my back as she sings. Taps would get a little quicker if you didn't fall asleep fast enough! From when I was a child, I can still remember the songs she used to sing to me. Part of our past that I cherish, and I recently found some of the songs on the internet. As soon as I heard them, I was transported back. One song is "Lulla Lulla, Bye Bye," which I sing to my children. My aunt also sings this to her grandchildren, the youngest is just six months old now and never got the privilege of meeting her great-granny - she was born five weeks after granny passed away, but we will be sure to tell her everything about granny and continue singing lullabies just like she would have done.

Things have changed so much over the years here. Community, people, attitudes. It's hard. Some of it is good, some not so good, and some bad. Granny's time won't come back and we've lost some of that importance of place that her generation had. Walker has had a massive regeneration over more recent years. Many properties were demolished and haven't been rebuilt. It destroyed communities and people lost their homes. We don't know who our neighbours are now and when I was younger, not that long ago, we all knew one another. I remember the millennium new year and we were all in each other's homes, front doors open and welcoming. We could never do that now. We used to leave our front doors unlocked, trusting the community, but my door is always locked these days.

We never see police patrolling the areas. I understand there are cutbacks and a lack of resources but we used to know the local beat officers and they would be present. There was something about knowing this that put the community at ease. We felt protected, secure, and people respected the authority. Now, it's invisible, dissolved and the lack of presence is felt. Cars are broken into, and strangers walk into people's homes to commit crimes, it's heard of weekly here now. There's a lack of services in general and this has deteriorated over the years. It's impacted the community, specifically around mental ill health. We have had some tragic deaths in the community, with young people taking their own lives. There are limited services for 13-19-year-olds in particular. Although some charities and services exist, there isn't enough. When I was that age, there was so much going on. It connected us and socialised us. Community centres allowed us to learn, develop confidence, and still have fun. There isn't enough now and kids are on computers, out and about committing anti-social behaviour or putting themselves in vulnerable positions. Crime has escalated, with an increase in gangs, violence, knife crimes, and organised crimes. My son is at an age when he wants to start socialising more with his friends, such as going to the shops and fast food restaurants. It's something I won't allow and not sure at what age I will feel comfortable with my kids doing their own thing.

It feels like the heartbeat of the community beats weaker and it's sad. But amongst this we have positives. New shops and amenities to help support the community. We never had a supermarket, just a small shop and people had to travel to the next town to get a big food shop. We now have a supermarket and other facilities that have made life easier for our community. Walker gets a bad name, but there are some great parts of the area. Women in Walker are still strong, bold, and determined. Women are heard more and attitudes have changed perceptions of women. Not everyone has these views, there are still many people who see women in certain roles in society. We remember where we have come from, and the struggles and strengths of the past. I hope those attitudes and appreciation will continue to be passed on to the younger generations for a very long time.

Hayley Webster, aged 38.

Dedicated to our granny, our Queen (Emily Jane Cox 1928-2023).

Finding my Place

My earliest memory was the birth of my sister in 1957, when I was two and a half years old. We lived in Scotswood and I remember the traumatic environment of the home birth as Mam went into labour two months early. There wasn't the equipment we have today, no incubators – instead, there were tiny hot water bottles tied around the inside of a crib to help keep the premature baby alive. The labour began with my mam saying she had a little bit of a pain in her back, quickly followed by a kerfuffle as it registered she was going into labour, the tension rising as her contractions grew stronger. The labour only took 20 minutes before my sister, Lynn, arrived into the world. I remember peeping around the open bedroom door where my mam was giving birth. I couldn't see her, just her legs on the bed and I recall them being a bit hairy! Then I heard an adult voice, harshly directed at me,

'She shouldn't be here, get her away.'

I didn't think about it at the time, I was only a child but that statement impacted my relationship with my sister. As she was coming into the world, I heard this line and felt like I shouldn't be there. Feeling that I was in the way and that Mam didn't want or need me anymore. It was the start of a whole life exploration for acceptance, sometimes to the point of compromising integrity and never really feeling that I quite fit in.

After Lynn was born premature, naturally she was vulnerable and needed extra attention and care. As an adult, I understand this but as a child, I felt pushed out and dismissed. It meant that as I grew up, I quickly became autonomous with limited interaction from Mam as Lynn needed more. I loved Mam deeply but it was a difficult dynamic at home. She never had a "normal" relationship with Dad, who fathered both Lynn and me. He was never fully on the scene. Dad was married and wouldn't leave his wife so the family dynamics were dysfunctional from the start. After I was born, at around six weeks old, Mam returned to work. My grandma, who was tiny but mighty, brought me up much of the time. When Lynn was born, Mam stayed off work for a year to care for her due to her fragility. Although necessary, as a child I felt like a discarded toy, replaced by a shiny, new one. Dad would come and visit but it wasn't enough and it must have been heart-breaking for Mam at times knowing he had another life that was more important than us. Dad was like the "posh man" that came to the house. He would give us gifts, attempting to buy our love or perhaps erase guilt with money.

When I was 19 years old, I became pregnant and Dad walked out of my life. He asked Mam to make a choice between him and me, wanting Mam to throw me out of the family home for becoming pregnant. He didn't even live there and had no right to pass judgement given his life choices. Mam told him to leave and not come back. That was it – the strange relationship I had with my dad was over, the door closed and forever bolted. He was dead a few years before I even found out and I grieved for the much craved loving father-daughter relationship I never had, more than for the man I never really knew.

As adults, Lynn and I have a relationship. We have always been different but she is my sister and I will always care for her. Mam died almost 40 years ago, when I was in my 20s. I remember as she was dying, going to her house. Cramming in visits before and after work and around caring for my daughter, Melanie. Ensuring Mam had something to eat, was clean and had taken her medication, as I watched her fade before my eyes. Lynn lived with Mam but was depressed and struggled with the inevitable demise of our parent. As Mam was admitted to the hospital, on the pathway to death, I remember rushing from work to see her every night. We would talk but every time the doors on the ward moved, she would look in case it was Lynn. Mam loved me, I know she did but I struggled with the relationships in our household growing up, feeling at times I was watching family love from the periphery. I know Mam didn't mean it, she knew that I was strong. I was, yet still a child and I didn't have all the answers, just like I don't have now.

As a child, I went to Denton Road Primary School. I was a very clever child and in school I thrived, feeling appreciated and supported in the first part of my education at least. As I got older, I passed my 11+ and went to the grammar school, Rutherford High School. Here, it became more apparent that I wasn't the same as the other children and was an easy target. Different because I was very studious and academic and different because I came from this strange family dynamic with Dad having another life. We had Dad's surname but not Mam's. It wasn't normal in the 1950s and made me stand out when all I wanted was to blend in. I began lying to fit in and be the same as my peers. I didn't want to be dishonest, I just wanted acceptance. I was told that I would be around many more intelligent people at Rutherford High, but I still managed to excel and obtain high marks, resulting in being placed in the higher sets. This led to more shunning, I couldn't win and struggled constantly to be accepted and find who I was. It was almost impossible to talk to Mam about things as she was busy working or looking after Lynn. I decided in year three of high school to fail. I was aged 13 and I stopped working hard, my attitude changed and I joined a group of rebellious girls. I began going to discos, riding on the back of motorbikes and smoking. I felt some acceptance at last. I still achieved my exam results and awards at school but realised that being clever isn't a gift when you're from the wrong background. I have been able to study and appreciate education in later life, which I am grateful for.

After leaving school, I enrolled in a local college to complete business studies alongside Spanish and French. I enjoyed college and met a group of people that I clicked with, a piece in my jigsaw of acceptance. Alongside college, I was dating a local lad and we got engaged. I was only 17 years old but naive in my search for love. He became controlling and abusive. It resulted in me not completing my studies after he coerced me into thinking I needed a job and education was wasted. I loved him, it was a love I needed and craved, even as it turned dark. I eventually had the courage to leave, knowing that it would never get better. By this time, I worked for an insurance company, enjoying the work but always searching for something extra, more to keep me stimulated. I saw an advert for hotel workers in what was then West Germany as the Berlin Wall was still an existing structure. I completed the application along with my friend, Sue. The next thing we knew, we were on a train to London, a ferry to Holland, and then a train right across to West Germany. I had never been out of the country before and it soon became a big adventure.

My job was as a chambermaid in a local motel and although I didn't speak a word of German, I soon picked it up. Sue and I met people and made great friends. Another rare pocket in my life so far where I could be myself. The people were lovely and included many Turkish people, who had settled in West Germany after the war to help the country rebuild. There were also Yugoslavians, Americans, and European students, making their way around Europe. It was hard work but such an experience with new people, cultures, and feeling free. I made a great friend, Dave, who was a 6'4", post-grad student from Alabama. He talked me into packing a bag and going hitchhiking. I left the security of my job and off we went! Dave and I stayed in some beautiful places throughout Germany and Austria. One day we went to the train station in search of room advertisements. We met a wonderful lady called Frau Arnol who offered us some space - a lovely room with a living area and bathroom. She was a widow and baked delicious cakes for us. We stayed for around a week, not realising until we left that she had been sleeping in her kitchen, whilst she gave us the rest of the property to make ends meet.

Dave and I continued on our travels until we reached Basle where he decided he wanted to go one way and I wanted to go the other, to Luxemburg. This was to visit Pete, a guy I knew from the college course I attended when I was 16 years old. I remembered his address so off I went, saying goodbye to Dave. I was 18 years old with my massive backpack, travelling solo in a new place. I reached what I thought was Pete's home but two elderly ladies lived there. Apparently, this address existed in every district and I was in the wrong district! However, these kind ladies invited me in. I washed and then they gave me a beautiful meal before arranging a taxi to take me to the right district, to Pete's home. We had a lovely few days before I decided it was time to hitchhike home. I managed to secure a lift with a lorry driver. We were both talking away in German to one another before he asked where I was from,

'Ich bin aus Newcastle,' I said.

He looked at me and started laughing before replying, 'Bloody hell, I'm from Wales!'

It wasn't long until we were back in the UK, arriving in Dover. My Welsh friend found me another lorry that was heading north. This one wasn't going all the way to Newcastle but took me to the next major city, where I disembarked and found another ride from a Dutch pop group. I stayed with them for about four days in their vehicle which was like the Scooby Doo van! It was certainly an adventure. My final lift home was in a brand new Rolls Royce with a salesman who had to deliver the car to Newcastle. He was an older man who had a daughter my age and I remember he was furious with me getting in the car, saying he would have been terrified if his daughter had done that. It made me realise that I never had anyone to stop me doing these things, despite any possible danger. But the man was lovely and he brought me home safely.

Resettling back in Newcastle, I secured a job in the Telephone Managers Office in a clerical role. I was quickly promoted and I met another group of people who were very "hip." They were lovely folk and took a lot of drugs at the time, introducing me to LSD and making cannabis available. I met Melanie's dad, Danny, through the group and became very rebellious, leaving my job. Danny and I remained in a relationship until Melanie was four years old. We had a council house in Scotswood, where you could always get a house at that time. I had jobs in the local supermarket, Dolcis shoe shop, and an accountant's office. After Danny and I split up, I continued working in the accountant's office and met someone else, through work. We had a three or four-year relationship and it was a normal, functional relationship without drugs and alcohol. However, I think we were both not quite mature enough for the relationship to progress. I loved him deeply and still think of him today. When this relationship ended, I was around 28 years old and Melanie was nine years old. I quickly met someone else and the relationship was rushed. We married and then soon had our daughter, Ruth. My husband wasn't well, he was a diagnosed paranoid schizophrenic and life with him was extremely difficult, leading to me having to leave when Ruth was three years old. Like Melanie, Ruth has a positive relationship with her dad. We just weren't right for each other as a couple. I still searched for acceptance and more pieces in my jigsaw but it felt like I had a history of meeting the wrong men. There was more judgement in those days towards failed relationships and single mothers but I was so blessed to have my daughters.

In the mid-1990s, I married a man called Bernard. This time it was right and Bernard loved the girls and accepted me. When I met Bernard, I had left the accountancy firm and had also worked for Traidcraft. However, I decided I wanted to return to study and I attended college, studying English language, social sciences, and quantitative methods before applying to university. I was lucky enough to be offered a placement at Durham University to study Linguistics, Theology, and Philosophy of Education. Bernard and I got married halfway through my studies and I took a year out of university after Bernard suffered a heart attack. I returned to my studies after 12 months and eventually graduated in 1995 before starting a teaching role in a local primary school. It was a lovely job and the children were wonderful but my ghosts of not feeling enough haunted me. I didn't always feel that I fitted in and would work excessively. It wasn't sustainable and I left the role with sadness but with an important reflection from the children - to never write off what you don't understand and to always try and find the meaning behind what someone is trying to express.

I moved onto a role at the church in 1998, I wasn't ordained and didn't wear a collar but I worked with the church offering support as a community church coordinator. My role allowed me to work in the local area with the community. I was there to support but not enforce religion. I have a faith and I'm still searching for the right components for me personally.

However, life took me off my path temporarily when I was 45 years old. It was 2000 and I was at an appointment at my GP's. She mentioned there was a pilot scheme offering mammograms to women between 40-50 years old. She asked me if I wanted to be involved and I agreed, not thinking anything else of it. I was invited to the local hospital and a mammogram was performed. It transpired I had breast cancer, a tumour less than a millimetre from my chest wall. It wouldn't have been detected by touch and I would never have had those visible symptoms to stop its' destruction. They advised me that six weeks later and it would likely have been terminal. One week later I had a mastectomy. No warning and no time to absorb the information and prepare myself. Following the surgery, I received treatment of radiotherapy for 25 weeks, with Bernard by my side throughout.

I returned to work after my treatment. At the time there had been an influx of asylum seekers into the UK. There were ten regions for dispersal, Tyneside being one of the identified areas. We had many people arriving, seeking safety. Most of the people were from Iraq as this was the time when Saddam Hussein was at his political height. We also had people from Iran, Afghanistan, Rwanda, Sudan, Ethiopia and Eritrea, to name some. The asylum seekers were all accommodated in hard-to-let properties but there were limited resources for support. One day, I was working in the office at the church when there was a knock at the door. Two men stood in the doorway, shivering. One was from Zimbabwe and the other was from Iraq. They had seen the church, hoping for sanctuary. I gave them some clothes and food and we found them accommodation. From this, the asylum seeker project began. With local churches and community development teams, we founded what became the East Area Asylum Seeker Support Group. We supported many people and hopefully made a difference. These people had nothing, everything had been stripped away; identity, family, friends, community. Many were left destitute and their asylum-seeker application, rejected. Other workers and me often had people staying in our homes who were destitute. The North of England Refugee Service would phone and ask for help – I couldn't say no. These were people's daughters, sons, and parents. I still keep in touch with some of them today and it's wonderful to see them thriving.

Bernard supported me throughout my career and we had a wonderful life together, albeit for only 12 years of marriage as Bernard wasn't well, suffering an aneurysm and a stroke. I remember him lying in the neuro-science block at the Royal Victoria Infirmary when he first had his stroke. He could speak but had no movement in his body except for one finger. Ruth was there and we were talking about when she was a baby. Bernard mentioned that he could remember taking her in his arms and she used to suck his cheek until it was red raw. He said how it always made him feel like she was his biological daughter, that he was her dad. I remember with such fondness that Ruth looked at Bernard and told him that he had always been her dad. We all loved him so much. After Bernard passed in 2005, I didn't want another relationship and I continued focusing on my work as I processed my grief.

I worked with asylum seekers for nine years before doing a Master of Professional Studies around the topic. Then in 2013, still employed by the Methodist Church, part of my job was to conduct a community chaplaincy at Pottery Bank Community

Centre. I also became a member of the charity's board and got more involved with the services at the centre. I set up a debt advice project that I am still involved with but is now supported by other people. I retired in 2021, however, I have never really left. I became involved with the Walking in the Footsteps of Walker Women project as I know many of the locals but I am hoping to retire fully after this.

I met my current husband, Paul, at a conference in Rotterdam in 2003. The conference was for community church workers across Europe and we became good friends. I remember it being the end of the first day and the group were meeting for an evening meal. There was one seat left, next to Paul. I sat down and we began talking, discussing the first day. I commented that it had been good but there were too many vicars and that they couldn't keep out of anything! I asked him what he did and of course, he replied with,

'I'm a vicar.'

Paul was there as he didn't have community workers attached to the church so had to attend himself, from his parish in Nottinghamshire. We kept in touch and after Bernard died, we used to meet as friends every fortnight or so at a halfway point between our homes. One day, I received a message from him telling me he loved me. So after being friends for some time, it developed into a relationship. We married in 2011 and Paul came to live in the North East. We are very happy and I look forward to spending more time with him on my final retirement!

As an individual, I will keep working on myself. My agony of disjunction and not fitting in through life has felt like going through a very dark forest. At times there have been clearings, where I have been able to be myself. I've travelled through the dark jungle, hacking my way through the thick, dense vegetation and sometimes found pockets of light, of rest where I can be myself before returning to the dark until I find the next clearing. I'm not quite always in the light but I'm almost there and it's taken a lifetime. I hope in my retirement, I can keep searching for a place of complete ease and now perhaps a place where I just accept myself. I've brought my daughters up to be who they want to be and not follow the crowd, reinforcing that they should never be afraid of who they are. They have always shone and I am so proud of them. They have achieved so much as people, not only career-wise but as wonderful, inspiring women. I also have two step-children and four grandchildren between all of our children and I'm so grateful for them all.

I love Walker and have spent much of my career working in this area. Although I don't live in Newcastle now, Walker has a special place in my heart. I love its raw honesty, no tip-toeing around, just a community who are open and honest.

Residents have huge pride in their community and love for their family, children, and neighbours. There is a unique solidarity. People bicker of course, but when they need each other – they are there. It has a permanent feel about it, people aren't transient like they are in other areas. Once you are in Walker, you are always here and even if you leave, many people gravitate back. Community spirit, may have changed over time but has never died and hopefully never will.

Christine Carroll, aged 67.

Dedicated to my daughters, Melanie and Ruth; just the thought of them makes my heart sing!

The Lyrics of my Life

My parents were in their 40s and already had three teenagers when I was born in 1948. And it wasn't just me that came along, but also my twin brother, Peter. We arrived into the world on my oldest brother, Bill's 14th birthday and the rest of the clan consisted of sisters, Grace who was 16 years old and Lyn, who was 12 years old. We lived in Scrogg Road but a bigger house was now needed so we moved to another council property on Hexham Avenue, where we lived for over a decade.

Twins: Peter and me

Peter and I were a Catholic accident. Mam was 42 years old and the doctor told her it was the menopause. She soon realised it wasn't and we were born in May, just months before the NHS began. Home was happy and we were a close family where religion was important. Praying every night before bed and visiting church on a Sunday was non-negotiable. We were different from the rest of the kids on the street, who were mainly Protestant children and we had differing religious practices. One of these involved the holy days of obligation, where we would go to church in the morning and then have the day off school to engage in the religious occasion.

There were no TV's in those days, well certainly not in Walker, so music was the majority of our entertainment. Mam was the most beautiful soprano and Dad was a comic. Mam came from a musical family and my uncle Michael, who lived in the area, was a tenor. We would have concerts at home and all of us would perform. It was our entertainment, but much more than that, it was precious family time. Bill would teach Peter and me to sing and dance in preparation for our Saturday night tradition. Life was hard in many ways, for all families, but life was also good and it became even better when we got electricity! Church Street in Walker had bombed-out buildings and I remember rushing from school, past the aftermath of the Second World War, to get home and turn the lights on and off. It was so exciting! Before this, it was gas mantles but we always got by, it was normal and everyone worked hard to keep the home. Within our house, we all congregated in the kitchen – high-back chairs were in front of the fire and we would sit together as a family. Like many of the families around us, we were poor, but we always had one another.

Peter, Bill, and me

The first school I attended was Walker RC First School on Welbeck Road. Peter and I were in the same class in our first year and then the boys and girls were separated. Whilst at the infant school, each Friday, we twins would get dressed up in our cowboy and cowgirl outfits and sing the song our older brother had taught us. My brother, Bill would take Peter and me to Walker Swimming Pool from being three years old. I loved it, feeling at one with the water and eventually swimming for the school and winning awards. I thrived around sports and excelled at each sport I participated in; football, cricket, and any others I could get involved with.

Everything that was associated with being a girl, wasn't for me!

Sport was an escape and something I could focus on. There were issues in the neighbourhood I lived in – sexual abuse in the community that became a local, abusive predatory ring of older lads. I remember comments aimed at me as puberty began and my body changed. Statements about my breasts and older boys asking to feel them. Lads who would lure me into where they were hanging around such as a pigeon cree or the park and would try and touch me and get their penis out. There was also a local man, in his early 20s who was dating a friend's older sister. Looking back, I think he was using her to get to younger children like me but back then I had no idea about grooming. He sexually abused young girls in the area – abuse felt insidious in our streets. I also remember going to visit Grace during the school holidays. She lived in Wallsend and had a young family, so I would go and help her with the children. When I was around 11 years old, I had been to Grace's house for the day and was travelling home on the bus. A man came and sat next to me and placed my hand in his pocket on his erect penis. I didn't know what to do and terror made me freeze, as I sat, heart pounding in my ears. Eventually, I reached my bus stop and I got up to leave. He told me he would accompany me and take me to the park. Panic engulfed me as I disembarked the bus and he came with me, holding onto my hand. I thought about running to get away. Luckily, a police officer came towards us and the predator ran off. I sprinted home, distressed and told my parents. Dad was furious and left the house to search for the offender but never found him, despite us reporting it to the police.

Me as a young girl

Within our area, there was sexual abuse within families, including those of friends in the street. Never in my family, but the predators in and around the estate preyed on their own family as well as others. As a girl, not quite a teenager, these were my first experiences of sexual interaction – abusive, intrusive, unwanted, and traumatic. It inhibited me socially, I was terrified of people and also didn't want people to find out what had happened to me. It led me to pretend I didn't know anything about sex and boys. The girls at school would sit me down and try and "educate" me. I would blush and they assumed I was naïve. I let them think it, the alternative felt unbearable. I remember the last year of school, two sisters had moved to live in our street. They found out what had been going on within the estate and began talking about it at school. I carried all the feelings typical to "victims," shame, guilt, and self-blame, not realising at the time that I was in no way, shape, or form responsible or accountable for the depraved, abusive behaviours of the perpetrators that lived in our community. I didn't want my parents to know and I panicked about the truths circulating. There were new houses available in another part of Walker. I planted the seed to my parents for us to move and it worked. I got out, away from the sexual abuse at the age of 14 years old.

I was quiet at school and didn't have a lot of friends, struggling to fit in with the girls in my class as I grew older. I did have a friend called Margaret, who attended a local youth club. I had spent over a year in the house after we moved, scared of any predators outside. Eventually, I went to the youth club with Margaret, making new friends and building my confidence. I got involved with all their sports and won their sportswoman of the year award when I was 15 years old – a much-needed boost. I had failed the 11+ at school in 1959 and left education at the age of 15 years old, with no qualifications after our whole class was told by the teachers that none of us were intelligent enough to be put forward for the Northern Counties Exam. After leaving school, I worked at the local Co-op in Byker. I loved it and ended up transferring to the Walker Co-op where I set up a food delivery service for older people.

Around this time, my mam's health deteriorated. She had been ill a lot during my life, but during this period she began demonstrating strange behaviours such as going shopping with odd shoes on. We would laugh and not think much more of it until it began occurring more frequently. I spent a lot of time looking after her, unclear of what was actually wrong. Keeping the home, food shopping and cooking – I would run upstairs to get instructions from her to create the planned meal for the evening. By this time, I had left the Co-op and was working in an office in town. One Saturday after a morning shift, my boyfriend, Johnny, collected me on his scooter and brought me home. Dad was at the club and Mam was in her dressing gown in the living room. Peter was there going mad, saying Mam was acting bizarrely. I called the doctor and Mam was admitted to the hospital in a toxic confusional state. It transpired she had a genetic disorder where her liver stored iron, rather than processing it and the confusion was due to liver cirrhosis. She was detoxed in the hospital and became well again, as much as she could with other health conditions.

I carried a lot of household duties for many years when Mam was poorly. My older sisters were in their own homes, Lyn having moved to Australia. I had been a feminist from an early age, around five years old when I remembered having to do the dishes and Peter never did! It was frustrating and whilst I would do anything for my family, it was hard work.

Me and Peter

Mam and Dad

In 1969, Mam died. I was 21 years old and Dad had retired by this point. Peter and I had been talking about getting a flat together but he changed his mind, wanting to live with a friend. I was working at a pub in town and Dunlop, as a sales ledger clerk. I had made friends with people at the pub who were going to London to live. They asked me if I wanted to join them. It was a way for me to leave everything I knew in Walker; the good and the bad. I wanted to experience life and although it sounds cliché, I really did need to find myself, for so many reasons! London could surely help with that – a few hundred miles away in distance but at the time, millions of miles ahead regarding the culture, community, and opportunity compared to the suburb I lived in. Grace was happy to look after Dad, so the decision was made and off I went to experience life.

I stayed in London for around ten months working in an accounts department at an insurance company. I loved the job and the organisation valued my brain, encouraging me and assisting me to develop my skills. Although happy in my job, I was never happy in myself, despite London being a cosmopolitan hive of activity. It was because my identity was muted. I'd always known I was a lesbian but had never been able to be myself. I remember at the youth club, years before, wanting to kiss a girl and being upset at myself for feeling that way. I didn't want to admit my sexuality and I suppressed my emotions, concreting them into a wall that was to never be knocked down. The cracks started in time. Before that, my boyfriend, Johnny, became my husband. He had remained in Newcastle when I was in London and I would travel up to see him and my family. One time I needed to return to London and the buses were on strike. My brother, Peter was now a singer-songwriter and told me Lindisfarne were travelling to London in their van – I could go with them! They weren't famous at this point and I travelled with them and received tickets to their gig that night. However, the gig didn't go ahead and the five band members came back and stayed in our flat for the night! I told one of the members I was getting married and he said,

'Don't get married and read The Female Eunuch, instead.'

I did get married and I also read The Female Eunuch, which left a lot to try and process.

Before getting married, I suggested Johnny and me should move in together on my return to London. But to live together, his condition was that we got married. I agreed, with stipulations for the wedding including not wearing a white dress, getting married at the Civic Centre, and him finding us accommodation. We were married, and moved into a bed-sitting room in a property in Jesmond, with some shared facilities. Johnny and me were married for eight years and got on really well, I loved my life with him but I was lying to myself about what I wanted and needed. I would continue to suffocate my sexuality, ignoring my reality. But my feelings and truth would come out to him when I was drunk and I would subsequently apologise.

Back home in Newcastle, when I first got married to Johnny, I continued working in accounts. One office based in Gosforth was close to the psychiatric hospital, St. Nick's. The patients would often wander in and I would be the member of staff who communicated with them. One day, I saw an advertisement for psychiatric nurses, based at the hospital. I had no qualifications but could apply for and sit the General Nursing Council exam. There were two courses available as an outcome, RMN and SEN, depending on the score. If 85% or higher was obtained, students could attend the three-year RMN course. I was invited to receive my results and they were over 85%! I couldn't believe it, the first time I had passed an exam and with a high score. I began the RMN course at the age of 25, working at the hospital and studying at the same time, earning and learning. During this time, I had begun attending the Women's Liberation Group in Newcastle. I used to visit London and explore literature and whilst there, I had bought a leaflet called The Social Construction of Women. I brought it home and couldn't understand a word of it. I asked a psychology student on the ward I was working on during my training to help me comprehend it. She spent hours reading it and writing it in layman's terms. The Women's Liberation Group was fantastic. With lesbians there, it felt like the home my sexuality had been searching for. At last, I had found my people.

By the end of the training, I hated psychiatry. It was the 1970s and treatment included heavy drugs and ECT. There was only one job I wanted and it was as a staff nurse in the drug and alcohol treatment unit where the patients were treated through psychotherapy. I applied and was successful. No uniforms were worn, everyone did the same work and we were all supported. I learnt so much in the role and each day, I facilitated psychotherapy groups with complex and sometimes violent people. The job was great and it was here that I came out for the first time in my employment history. I worked in the role for around two and a half years before I was ready for something different. I was still living with Johnny at this point. We loved one another and had always been so close. I would attend Reclaim the Night marches and he would help to make banners for the women to carry. I then met a woman, a student nurse, who attend the Women's Liberation meetings with me. We ended up in a relationship. She had been two weeks away from getting married and subsequently cancelled the wedding. I eventually admitted my sexuality sober and left Johnny. Even though it was hard for him, Johnny supported me as did my family and even Johnny's mother.

I was becoming more and more myself as time went on, comfortable at last as if my skin fit me for the first time. I wanted to do more for feminism and my early experiences of sexual abuse and violence, along with the experiences of other women, eventually led me to be part of establishing the Rape Crisis Centre in Newcastle in the late 1970s. A team of around 30 women, we would complete training including how to counsel and support people who would be accessing the service. I recall one time, watching a video and the content was around what happens to young people if they are victims of sexual abuse whilst they are at school. It was almost like watching my own life, repeated back to me on the screen. I was determined to help victims and we did, as a collective.

I had a big circle of female, lesbian friends. One of them, Maggie, used to play the guitar and we would all harmonise. Four of us; Maggie, Lesley, Elaine, and I started hanging around together. It was 1979 and we established a band called Friggin' Little Bits, officially in 1980. We wrote unique songs about misogyny, politics and being lesbian, such as Dykes Delight and The Country Song. Friggin' Little Bits travelled the UK and abroad, singing to female-only audiences. An album was made and we are still on Spotify. It was an incredible time and we performed in so many wonderful venues to phenomenal women. Our music and message were something different, something powerful, giving women a voice and empowering women to be themselves, standing up against the patriarchy. We even appeared in a film, shown on Channel 4, with a snippet of the band being shown again in the late 1980s on the tv programme Points of View, encouraging lesbian media to be played before the watershed! The fun eventually came to an end and the band split up. However, in the 2000s, we reunited, wrote some more songs and performed for women and gay men, before retiring for good.

Whilst in the band, I continued to work in a variety of roles including a job at a place called The Children's Warehouse and working with carers of people with dementia. In this latter role, I was advised to do my social work training for future job opportunities. I began studying and once qualified, I got a job as a service co-ordinator at Richmond Fellowship. It was a new service, needing to establish and develop housing for people with mental ill health as the psychiatric hospitals were closing. It was around 1990 and I started a role as acting area manager, also covering services in Manchester and Wakefield, alongside the North East. After a while, a permanent area manager role came up but I didn't apply, not wanting to do the job any longer. My former role was obsolete and therefore, I was made redundant.

Friggin' Little Bits (me on the right)

Next on the jobs carousel was a role as a lecturer at Newcastle College in health and social care. I had much experience of training but had never taught lectures, so trained for the CertEd. I worked there for around 6-7 years. I also studied for a counselling qualification. Newcastle College offered redundancy and I took the opportunity. Subsequently, I focused on my counselling, competing further training in psychotherapy before becoming registered with the UKCP. I then set up my own, private practice in Jesmond, offering psychotherapy and remained in this role until I retired. Throughout my career, I enjoyed all my jobs in different ways and each offered and taught me something. I thrived working with people and hopefully helped people in their times of need.

I've been with my wife, Chris, for over 30 years. We met in the mid-1980s and have been a constant since. Our life together has been filled with mutual support, friendship, and love and although she still works, we enjoy holidays and time at home together. I no longer live in Walker and have limited, distant family in the area. When I was younger, I felt I had to lose Walker to find myself. As time went on and I lived in Jesmond, I had no roots left in Walker. My parents had both died and my siblings had left the area. There felt no place for me there but a big part of me feels I also didn't dare to be my true self there, or anywhere in particular in those days. I do still have fond memories of my family, good times in the home and lots of love. Sadly, Grace and Peter have now both passed, Peter only earlier this year. Bill is still alive, in his 80s, healthy and active and Lyn is still alive.

I spend my retirement gardening and reading. Chris and me recently visited Bali and Australia (to see my sister, Lyn). The lyrics of my life have been a colourful song. I'm grateful for how I have been able to live my life, even if it took a long time to be able to be myself. I have had adventures, opportunities, worked in great places, and met many magnificent people, and even though I don't live there now, Walker was where it all started.

Pat Scott, aged 75.

Flying Without Fear

In 1945 I arrived into the world, born into the community of Walker. From the age of two years old, my family and I lived at the bottom of Pottery Bank. It was a lovely place with great people and it had the most wonderful sense of community. There were two pubs, The Ellison and The Raglan and a wooden hut which sold groceries and sweets, ran by a mother and son set-up called the Lambs. Further along the road were the gated factory house and public toilets, as well as Jones's Piggery and the tar yards. Then at the top of the hill was a lookout with Curtis's Piggery, the shore and the Viking wreck also there. It was a place within a place, a real community where everyone helped one another out and smiles were plenty.

I wouldn't change my childhood for anything and I have many happy memories. I was one of five children, with an older brother, two older sisters, and a younger brother. We grew up close as a family but sadly, we lost one of my sisters, Elsie, when she was young.

There were many traditions in the days of my youth that are rather alien to most children now. For example, when I was a youngster, everyone went to church. It was part of people's routine and was expected, especially on a Sunday. These days, children visiting church seem to be the exception rather than the rule. We would go to St. Anthony's Church, which is now closed. It was always a great day and we genuinely enjoyed it as children. Our parents had attended church and their parents before them - my great, great-grandfather was the first verger at St. Anthony's Church.

Dad in the army   My mother

At home, things were hard for us and many families. We didn't have the convenience of much in life that we have today, but we were always fed and looked after. We had hens and my mother was an excellent cook. We never went without and often my mother would give eggs to the neighbours. There was an unwritten rule of looking out for one another, helping when needed. Solidarity in the community. My granny lived with us, as many grandparents did in those days, extended families were close by or in the same home. Granny used to wring the necks of the chickens, which I didn't like and tried not to witness.

Granny was a wonderful woman; modest and traditional. She had a big influence on me in many elements of my life, including that I am very private in lots of ways. Granny was born in 1877 and lived through both WWI and WWII, living until 1957, at almost 80 years old. The other strong woman in my life, my mam, passed in 1980 and my dad died in 1990.

The Mother's Union in the late 1940's – early 1950's.

I attended West Walker School and enjoyed my education on the whole. I was a mischievous and cheeky child, with lots of personality. The day I turned five, in July 1950, I wanted to go to school.

My mother told me I had to wait until after the summer holidays to start in September. I wouldn't wait and insisted I had to begin my education. So along we went after I rejected my mother's offer of a September school start. The next day, I ran away from school! I found out that the class were expected to lie on mats for an afternoon nap. I refused to and I was placed in a corner by the teacher, Miss Marshall for disobeying. However, the corner was close to the classroom door, so I scarpered as fast as my little, five-year-old legs could carry me. I ran along the street and Miss Marshall had to chase me, catching me and carrying me back to school as my legs kicked the air in defiance.

Another time at school, I got accused of talking, when I wasn't. The teacher threw a board duster at me, which they were allowed to do in those days. I was fuming as I hadn't been talking, I had been doing my work as instructed. So I threw the board duster back at the teacher. It didn't go down well!

I was very headstrong as a child and knew my own mind. I was a tomboy and playful and my mother was often called into the school to discuss my latest shenanigans. I used to hang around with the lads from Pottery Bank housing estate and get up to all sorts. My role was often as a lookout and I would watch, monitor, and get ready to call out to the lads to run, as they stole turnips from the allotments. We always had lots of laughter and fun. However, when I was 11 years old and started senior school, the tomboy in me started to dissolve. I became more feminine and I developed closer relationships with my female school and neighbourhood friends.

I remember wanting to leave education and go to work. At 13 years old, I visited the careers advisor at school who granted me a work permit to work part-time alongside my education. I began a weekend job at Woolworths. It was amazing and I also got the chance to work in school holidays, experiencing work and earning money. My job used to pay me 7 and 6 in old currency. I would work on the tills, or the counters serving biscuits or sweets. I remember working on the ice cream machine, which I really enjoyed. It was incredible getting a wage!

When I eventually left school, I started work at St Anthony's Co-op. I was offered work at an office through school but office work didn't appeal to me. The school sent me for an interview and I was successful, ready to start the role the following Monday. It wasn't for me, as predicted, and I ended up swapping roles with another girl in the drapery, who was pregnant and wanted a less hectic position. The drapery allowed me to be more front-facing with customers, which I preferred. After this job, I worked in factories, deciding I wanted to work more

Monday-Friday shifts so I could go out socialising with my friends.

On weekends we would go to the local dances. On a Wednesday we frequented Heaton to dance, Friday nights, we would attend the Oxford and again sometimes on a Saturday. Then on a Sunday, we would visit the Embassy at Forest Hall. I adored dancing, especially rock n roll. It was something we all did as friends and it kept us fit. The music was uplifting and upbeat and we became quite good movers!

I danced most of my life and I remember one occasion with my sister-in-law and lifelong friend, Ann. My late husband, John, had been in the army and we all attended an event near Reading. Ann and me got up to dance. There was just us on the dancefloor, no one else. Our own space on view to everyone but we had a great time, like it was just us in the room, thoroughly enjoying ourselves. I danced up until I was 61 years old when I had a heart attack and knew I had to slow down a little. But I treasure the memories of dancing, where my body would come alive to the beat of the music. When I experienced my heart attack, my life changed as it often should when these illnesses and second chances happen. I had a stent fitted and I stopped smoking immediately. Returning home after my operation, John had cleared the house of any cigarettes. I never went back to smoking and I was grateful life had given me another go. I have angina now and I get the odd twinge but on the whole, I am doing well and feel healthy.

John was the older brother of Ann. I knew him but had little to do with him and no interest in boys when I was at school. John was six years older than Ann and me and he worked in the local butchers. He then joined the army and I remember being around 13 years old and he had returned home on leave. John had been stationed in Malta and came back to Walker with a lovely tan. That's when I first really noticed him and thought about how handsome he looked! He was a Gunner in the army and like most men of that generation after he left the armed forces, he didn't really talk about his time serving. We did, however, travel to Malta when we were married, visiting where he had been stationed.

When I was 16 years old, John asked me out. I thought my mother would kill me as he was 22 years old at that point. I was reluctant but then when I was 17 years old, I was hospitalised with my appendix and he knocked at my parents' house and asked if he could go and visit me in the hospital. He was invited to my parent's home for tea and approval. Luckily for us both, they approved and that was that, John and me were official. My family loved John after that meal and he became one of us.

John used to tell the story to the grandkids of when he came to tea for the first time at my parents' home. He couldn't believe the amount of food on the table. A melody of home-cooked, baked treats. Everything you could imagine as if a whole party was about to start. Food covered the table, all sorts on offer, guaranteed to fill a stomach and offer an explosion to the tastebuds. I can't understand how my mother managed to fit everything in — looking after us, keeping the home, and all the cooking. Each Sunday we would have a cooked breakfast, a Sunday roast dinner, and never-ending baked pies, tarts, quiches, and bread. She was amazing and many women in those days managed so many responsibilities as naturally to them as breathing.

John and me on our wedding day in 1964

John and me celebrating our 50th wedding anniversary

John and me were courting until we married on my 19th birthday. We had many happy years of marriage together, but I wish we had longer. John was a great man and a wonderful father and grandfather. We have two sons and a daughter. Our oldest son, Steven is 58 years old, followed by John who is 57 years old and our daughter, Lynne is 48 years old. All our children live locally, in Tyne and Wear. Apart from eight years when John and me moved to Widdrington, in Northumberland, I have always been in Walker. When we moved further up north, we lived in a stunning cottage with views of the sea and farmer's fields all around. It was a beautiful place but it wasn't us, despite being the image of tranquility we returned to Walker. It's home, where I'm from and where my heart has always been.

Life with John was magnificent and we used to do a lot together. We had ups and downs, as with every relationship. But we were a team and we always said goodnight to one another at the end of the day, regardless of what may have happened that day. That's one of the secrets to a happy marriage, in my view. He knew everyone and would speak to people wherever we went, always being friendly and trying to help others. We would go to the local pub, have nights out, and enjoy holidays away. I used to be terrified of flying so John and me used to travel to Europe by coach. Some of the journeys were so long and it would feel like it was taking forever to get to our destination. It was more tolerable when we were younger but as we aged, it was becoming less appealing to travel in a coach for up to 24 hours to get to begin our holiday. We visited Hungry, Italy, Austria, and more places by coach but it was just too much as we began to age. So I agreed to try flying again for our holidays, hoping that it just wouldn't happen. We had a caravan in Sandy Bay for 20 years and all of our friends were talking about going away for Christmas, abroad. I came in from work on the Monday and John had booked it for us. I did have to consume quite a bit of vodka to get me through the flight and I clung to John throughout, gripping him in sheer terror. So although we were no longer travelling in a coach for hours on end, poor John had a few bruises on his arm after each flight!

I have flown ever since. It's strange as the day that John died, I was holding his hands and I could feel this indescribable strength coming out of him, soaking into me. It was surreal and I can recall it like it was yesterday. The strength came out of his hands as I held them, knowing he was fading like the summer sun as it got closer to the end of his life. I have been able to get on a plane since, with no drama or anxiety. It's bizarre, but I feel like he passed on the courage before he died, dissolving my fear. Perhaps in his own way of wanting me to continue with life and not miss out on the holidays we loved so much. I've flown with friends and on my own since and it feels normal, not terrifying like it did all those years.

John passed in November 2016, aged 77. He was a young, fit 77-year-old until his health deteriorated. He used to walk all over, always out and about, active and motivated. Three weeks before he was diagnosed with cancer, he was told by medical professionals that apart from having a hiatus hernia, he was a fit man. Then within a month, he was diagnosed with pancreatic cancer. John started losing weight and began to deteriorate, fading slowly before me. He tried to keep upbeat but didn't want people to see his decline. We were married for just over 52 years when he passed. You never get over a loss like that, you just adapt and cope as much as you can.

For all John was six years older than me, I never thought he would die before me. I've learnt to live with my loss and John not being here – an empty place around me where he should be. It took a long time and I still struggle on occasion, losing a love like that will never be something you can heal from. At first, in the early days, I couldn't sleep and it felt like I would never recover. I still tell John off for leaving me, he's such a massive void in my life.

I have a good family, which helps. My children and grandchildren and great-grandchildren. I have eight grandchildren and nine great-grandchildren.

One of my grandchildren was born in March, on John's birthday, after he had passed. A strange thing happened before she was born – John came to me in a dream in the January of that year. I saw him standing in a doorframe in his younger years and he said,

'She's coming on my birthday at ten to one.'

I couldn't stop thinking about it the next day and I told my family about the dream. Then as the days in March passed, our granddaughter hadn't been born. It reached John's birthday and she was born at 12:59. Her shoulder became stuck whilst her mother was giving birth otherwise she would have been born several minutes earlier. It was a very strange but massively comforting to feel that John had been around.

As well as a wonderful family, I'm lucky that I have friends for support and companionship. Each Wednesday I go to a group through a local service and I go out each Friday night to a local venue, The Coronation Club. Here we play bingo, have a drink, and all catch up. After John passed, I didn't think I would ever go out on a night time again and it was a friend, Ann Simpson, who got me to venture out. Sadly, she died last year and is a big miss. Ann encouraged me to go on holiday with her to Benidorm and other places, she included me with her family and she was a precious friend. I also go away with my dear friend, Carol, to Lanzarote or

Benidorm. We always have a wonderful break and the change of scenery is good for us. Alongside my travel and going to my groups, I enjoy sudoku, crosswords, and watching TV. Life is good, even if my John is a massive miss.

I love living in Walker despite lots of changes over the years in the area, as well as changes in the country and world. As generations have passed, women's roles have changed. My mother was the housekeeper, cook, and carer. I was the same with John, his tea was ready on the table and the house was kept clean. I would cook everything, although John did make delicious soup. I wanted to do it, enjoyed those tasks and John was grateful. Things have changed today, roles are different and everyone does their share. Women shouldn't be expected to do everything in the home, but there are some things that I think we do better!

It used to be a lot safer on our streets and nowadays I wouldn't dare walk around at night, even sometimes through the day I am nervous. Knife crime, gangs of young people, it's tragic and dangerous. There are limited activities happening in the community for kids and not many places where they can go. I think this has a negative impact on youngsters as they are bored and everything is electronic. Imagination isn't used like it was. As children, we didn't have a lot of money but we enjoyed every minute of our time. We would dance, visit parks, and take picnics. We made the most of it and used our minds to create games and fun. It saddens me that children today are growing up in a dangerous society. I wouldn't want to be young in this day and age.

However, where I live now is great and I know all my neighbours. Unlike in the past, I ensure I lock my front door, you have to these days. Years ago, we could leave our front door unlocked all day and all night without fear that someone would come in to steal from us or attack us. We respected our elders, knew them and knew they would keep an eye on us. Neighbours were called Mr. and Mrs. - we had that courtesy. Don't get me wrong, people used to fight. They would fist fight, then shake hands. People seem to hold vendettas these days and use violence as a way to seek revenge. Life isn't valued. But the old Walker, the old community is still there in some ways, through the kindness of neighbours and memories being kept alive.

Irene Vout, aged 78.

Dedicated to my late husband, John and my late sister, Elsie.

The Value of Life

I've lived in the area of Byker and Walker all of my life. Born in Byker, we moved to neighbouring Walker when I was two years old. This was following the slum clearance initiative in Byker to demolish some of the old housing. Before it was demolished, my birth home was a two-roomed house, one room being a bedroom and the other the living area and kitchen area in one. Six of us, plus a dog all squashed into that tiny flat; my parents and four children. Mam was amazed when we moved to Walker, to a house that had an indoor bathroom and space.

Mam used to tell me about the flat in Byker. Getting to the toilet in the house sounded like an obstacle course! You had to go out the front and into the back lane to the rear of the flat. It was somewhat of a planned operation and if you left it too late, well there could be accidents. We shared the toilet with the people in the flat upstairs. For all the lack of space and amenities, Mam loved that flat and it took her a long time to settle in Walker when we moved. There was a history in that small, cramped, inconvenient flat that was etched into Mam's heart and stayed there, long after the bricks and dust were removed and something else was built in its place. She did however get very excited to have indoor plumbing in Walker, a full bathroom, two toilets, and central heating, as did Dad and us kids. Mam would go in her "kitchenette," which she adored and it took a while for her to get out of the habit of throwing the veg scraps on the fire – which was now electric! She was so used to doing it in the flat in Byker, onto the coal fire, keeping the fuel going. It was like another life had begun once we moved and a life Mam gradually settled into, grateful that she and Dad could bring their family up in an environment that wasn't as hard.

Out of us four siblings, I was the youngest with three, older brothers. My eldest brother, Ronnie, tragically died in a car accident. My dad was driving the vehicle at the time and it had a monumental impact on my family and my upbringing. Trauma like that never goes away and it haunted my family, in particular Dad, all his life. It changed who he was and it altered my mam. The devastating accident happened when I was only a toddler so I have no memories of my brother. However, I remember the atmosphere when Ronnie died – the crippling cloak of inconsolable sadness that my parents carried, heavy, weighing them down. That cloak became part of the uniform they wore all their life, the void for Ronnie never disappearing, never healing.

When the fatal accident happened, my Dad hadn't passed his test. He was a good driver but didn't have that rubber stamp approval document. This made him blame himself more and guilt became his shadow. However, the accident couldn't have been prevented by Dad, even if he had passed his test and was the best driver in the world. An articulated lorry ploughed into the side of the car and that's what killed my brother. Alongside Ronnie being in the car, one of my other brothers, Steve was also a passenger along with his friend. They both sustained injuries but recovered. Dad subsequently became very protective of us, especially over me and sometimes to smothering levels. He didn't like me going out and it was a constant battle in our house.

Grandad used to live not far from us, in Daisy Hill. I recall Mam asking me to pop over to Grandad's for something and Dad wouldn't let me go out of the street. Always in sight.

Mam with her siblings, Alice, Billy, and Georgie

In the 1960s and sadly still to a degree today, men never asked for help. Dad was prescribed tranquilizers but didn't talk about what happened to Ronnie and the pain of loss. Men didn't speak of their emotions, it was seen as a sign of weakness. No matter how much trauma you had experienced or how haunting and heavy the cloak you carried was they simply didn't talk and no one asked. Walls of silence. Mam lost her mother three months after we lost Ronnie. She had been so close to her mam, just like I was to her. Struggling, she suffered a breakdown. The house was filled with grief and Mam and Dad couldn't talk to each other about it even though they loved one another. The experience in many ways weakened them as a unit and Dad went on to have affairs in later life. We had family close to support us all, aunts and uncles who helped and became a listening ear, for Mam in particular.

I attended school locally, at Warrior Street. I enjoyed my education but I was very shy and got bullied – an easy target. Life was challenging with Dad's over-protective side. I used to be "resourceful" and go to my auntie Alice's, who moved up to Benton. Along with my cousins, we would go off for the day to Jesmond Dene and the surrounding area. I felt free there, like a bird in the sky, without Dad keeping me around the doors. I understood as an adult why he behaved in that way, but as a child, it was smothering and impacted my confidence. Dad was a good dad but in many ways, he was a selfish man in others, spending his money in the pub at times, rather than on his family and going on to be unfaithful to Mam.

Me (third from left) with my cousins and brothers.

Mam was a strong woman, but traditional. I remember each Sunday, she would cook a roast dinner. We would be starving hungry but we had to wait to eat until Dad got in from the club. Mam would check at the window every now and then, trying to spot him walking towards home so the food could be warmed and served. Waiting, patiently, as if for summer from a long, harsh winter.

I remember thinking that I didn't want a life like that when I was older. Although the women in those days were strong, having multiple roles and managing other people's lives - they would be the child-rearer, the cleaner, the cook, housewife, alongside many of them working. But they still kept in "their place," knowing that they were below the needs and voices of men. Growing up with two brothers, I knew it would be easy for me to turn out like Mam and my brothers to turn out like Dad. History repeating, recycled into the next generation. I adored Mam, but I didn't want my life to be like hers. I was a stubborn, little girl. Partly because it was me who was expected to go to the shops, set the table and do the chores, whilst my brothers sat on their backsides! It was difficult to challenge my dad, he didn't want to hear it and as I became a teenager, I became increasingly uncomfortable with the roles I was expected to do.

My parents, brothers, and me

When I started senior school, I was bullied a little but I soon developed my confidence and the targeting ceased. I then worked out that getting along with the teachers gave me the green light to get away with most things and that communication can greatly assist with negotiation! I was sporty at school, playing netball and football with a local community centre. Outside of school, I would go ice-skating and to discos, alongside camping with my cousins who I'm still close with today.

After leaving school at 16 years old, my first job was at Littlewoods on Northumberland Street in Newcastle. Then I moved to their warehouse in Walker and I loved it. I was around 18 years old and met a girl called June who became a good friend. June and I would go out on a weekend to the bars in town. I soon began dating the father of my children. We already knew one another as he lived in my street and got chatting one night on the bus returning from the pubs. We began dating but after a few months, I felt it wasn't working out and ended it. I soon changed my mind after seeing him with another girl and we reconciled, going on to have three kids. Our oldest, Karen is 40 years old, Steven is 38 years old and Kerry is 35 years old. However, as a couple, things fell apart for us after several years. We were very different with dissimilar priorities and the relationship dissolved.

Eventually, before Christmas, when my youngest child was around five years old, we split up. The children still have a good relationship with their father and we are amicable with one another. It took a long time to process the separation and there were a lot of issues, but life is calmer now. My focus was always on my children and we kept going as a little, loving unit. Even though my children are now adults and have their own children, we are still very close. Relationships impact children, both when they are good and bad. It's hard, but sometimes people who produce children just aren't suited and staying together isn't the best thing for the precious children involved.

After the relationship with the kid's dad ended, I had another long-term relationship which lasted around a decade. We got on well at first but alcohol became the third wheel in our relationship and as with so many people, being intoxicated brought a side out in my partner that I didn't like. The fate of the relationship was sealed when my mam was receiving end-of-life care and I was upset one night and he was drunk. When Mam died, I phoned my family and my friends, Jacqui and Sheila. He was last on the list to call and it made me realise, he wasn't important enough to me anymore, and likely I wasn't important enough to him. So our relationship ended along with the cans of beer he so quickly drank and tossed to one side. He's changed himself now and we are also amicable, people are just so often not suited as a couple.

My parents have both now sadly died. Dad died from cancer over 30 years ago and Mam passed away six years ago, just before Christmas, aged 84 years old. She suffered from dementia and was in a care home in the local area. I've had my own health problems, mainly experiencing a brain heamorrhage that occurred in my late 40s which changed my life. I was in the house and sneezed or coughed then felt something cold going through my head. I stood up to move to another room and my legs became weak. I began shaking with pain, not knowing what was going on. An ambulance was called and at first, it was thought I had trapped a nerve in my neck but the paramedics advised me to go to the hospital and get checked over. I reluctantly went, although I just wanted to go to bed and sleep. The hospital conducted a scan and I was subsequently advised I had a subarachnoid haemorrhage. The consultant stated that I had been lucky as 50% of people die from them. I was operated on and at first, it didn't work so further surgery was conducted on my brain. My thinking, both metaphorically and literally changed. I thought about life and what I wanted – it gave me such a wake-up call. Also since the haemorrhage my emotions can be hard to regulate and I cry easily and my short-term memory is impacted, meaning I can't concentrate for long. I struggle to read and can't do cross-stitch which I used to love. However, I'm alive and grateful every day for that.

Mam with her sister, Alice   Mam and Steve

A few years after Mam died I began a career in care. I had been working in retail and used to work for Woolworths until they went into administration. I spent some time working at a local supermarket, but didn't enjoy it then moved to Stagecoach buses. After I split up with my partner at the time, I needed a job with more income so I joined a local agency before deciding to join the care profession, especially after seeing Mam deteriorate and the care she received. I was employed by a local service supporting older people in a residential home. It's an extremely hard job that is undervalued. Care work is low paid, working long hours with poor terms and conditions a lot of the time, such as zero hours contracts or minuscule pension contributions. It is emotional, physically exhausting work and every carer holds a massive amount of responsibility for the health and welfare of each resident, including safeguarding. Sometimes carers are the only people in the world for those elderly residents, their everything.

My career as a carer commenced two years before the Covid-19 pandemic. When the pandemic started, I still worked in the field, now as a domestic in a care home. I won't ever forget the distress, fear, and trauma that along with the killer infection, soaked the air in the care home during those horrendous years. So many lovely, elderly people who we lost. So many hands that we held as the person died in pain, or fear, unable to be surrounded by loved ones. We became their loved ones – their families. We were their daughters and sons, there with them so they didn't die alone. I remember feeling that my heart had cracked into a million pieces, stamped on so many times, as I tried to comfort an elderly person with Covid, knowing all the while I was myself, at risk. Someone who was unlikely to survive and needed ease, reassurance, and a person to be there with them as they left the world.

My soul turned black during those long, painful, destructive years and I don't think the shadows that haunt me will ever truly go. They are buried deep, but every now and then, they make a sound or a movement and it all comes back to me. People will never know, never understand unless they experienced it. Sadly, far too many people did experience it and few people in the health and social care fields ever got real help to deal with and process a trauma that was something similar to a horror film. The added insult was that carers never got recognition during the multiple lockdowns. I've never met a carer who didn't feel like this. In many ways we got the scrag ends of gratitude, the end of the clap, and the bottom of the list of thanks alongside bin men. The whole team and people working throughout care homes did our best. With many dying in the process, dealing with death day in and day out as our own life ran on a hamster wheel of fear and uncertainty. All for minimum wage and what felt like minimal gratitude.

I remember holding laptops and phones for families to see their loved ones when they were poorly. A technological prison that they couldn't reach their mother, father, aunt, uncle, or grandparent through. Never knowing if that would be the last time they saw them on a screen. Unable to kiss them, hold them and often having to tell them all that they wanted to say in such an artificial, disturbing environment. Most of us aren't ever ready to lose someone, even when terminal illness snatches time we have left with someone and we see them fading in front of us. Like daffodils wilting and dying as the season changes, we are never truly ready to say goodbye. The pandemic made this a million times worse. For families losing someone and unable to hold them, comfort them, it was like being concreted in the sand watching someone drown in the sea, helpless. Instead, it was we as carers who took on family roles by proxy. A poor equivalent for a real relation, but the only choice everyone had. And although we weren't blood family, many of the elderly people in the care home felt like family and we loved each one of them.

When you spend 8-12 hours, five plus days a week with people, they become more than "clients." They are friends, family. We find out about them as individuals; their likes and dislikes, what makes them laugh, their past, and their vulnerabilities. We care for them and they rely on us. So even though we were that poor equivalent of their real family, we absorbed and carried the pain of grief for each person we lost over those few years and we still carry it now. Around 30 people died in the care home I worked at during the pandemic. Some of those who passed, I had worked with as a carer for two years (and still interacted with as a domestic). People were sent to the care home with Covid, it was a constant battle. We had limited PPE at first, like many care establishments. We always had aprons and gloves but obtaining masks was difficult at first.

Then wearing masks for 8-12 hours at a time impacted us all. The stock of PPE improved, but the impact of wearing it never did. People residing in the home who had dementia couldn't see our smiles of comfort under the masks, and although they protected our breathing system, I'm not sure they covered the fear in many of our eyes as we tried to do our job. I won't ever forget it, I can't, and I will carry it with me forever.

Me, working during the pandemic

Me, when Covid restrictions had eased

I remember the first time the reality of the pandemic hit me, like a kick in the stomach. The private ambulances in the car park would pull up, usually to take a deceased resident away. I remember seeing the paramedics covering up, putting full protective suits on in the car park before entering the building. Everyone was terrified, having to protect themselves. I recall getting home each night, taking my clothes straight off and immediately going to the bathroom to wash. I would cry in the shower, the water mixing with my tears, not knowing if it would ever end. Thinking how I could possibly help more and also swallowing the fear of contaminating my own family.

I remember a female resident who had Covid. One shift her buzzer went and she was choking on phlegm. We couldn't do anything, it was horrendous. The worst death we had ever seen. These situations occurred over and over, a living nightmare. This poor lady was buried with no one but the undertaker at her funeral, like so many people lost during that horrendous time. How do family members ever get over that? The answer is, they don't. It won't ever go away. Another time two residents died of Covid within a few hours of one another on different floors of the care home. A private ambulance arrived and a colleague opened the door asking if it was for one of the person who passed on her floor. The paramedic advised her it was for someone else and my colleague broke down. It was too much to absorb that people were just dying constantly. People who we all cared about so much. We had a lot of staff who couldn't cope with what was happening and went on the sick, some poorly themselves and some stressed, traumatised, and terrified. Counselling was offered at work, which was great but I was referred separately by my GP to Talking Therapies which was very helpful. I couldn't sleep and the specialist supported me, helping me to reduce my overthinking and manage the trauma. I was also prescribed anti-depressant medication.

The residential unit was massive and we had 13 domestics at the time. We ended up as a team of three as people went off sick. It meant kitchen staff had to help, all of us doing a bit of everything in a desperate attempt to keep the lifeboat of the care home afloat. Alongside this, we had the absolute unknown of what would happen and when it would all end to try and absorb. We would get texts when our shift ended, after returning home, shell-shocked, telling us another resident had passed. We were used to death, it happened in our field of work, but this was another level and death was accompanied by a heavy, painful fear.

At times there weren't enough staff and when a few residents were poorly at once, it made hell feel like a holiday camp. I could never talk about it at the time with my family – they would have locked me in the house and not let me go to work. My colleagues and I were going through something horrifyingly unique and I'm pleased we had each other, especially my friend, Irene, who at times kept me going and hopefully I did the same for her.

Sadness continued after the death of the residents where most items had to be bagged up into black bags and burnt, with little or nothing being kept and disinfected before passing to loved ones. I remember a little group of three residents who all used to sit together in the communal area. They had great banter and we would laugh together. They were adorable. One of them always thought she was going home and would pack her bags and carry them around. It was heartbreaking enough to see her with dementia. But she was always happy and had friends, especially the other two women in her little gang. They would brighten my shift. They all died during the pandemic through Covid. It was crushing, a tonne of bricks falling on my heart.

There was a Channel 4 dramatization on the TV called Help. It featured the brilliant Stephen Graham and Jodie Comer. The storyline was based around the pandemic in a care home and it was excellently written and acted. It showed, in my opinion, what it was really like. Everyone worked hard during the pandemic, across so many industries. Someone asked about our role as carers recently. I summed it up that we all worked hard during the pandemic, beyond hard in catastrophic conditions. The difference for us as carers was that the patients weren't nameless faces, people off the streets. They weren't that tragic conveyor belt of poorly people. They were people who we had spent 40-60 hours with a week. They were family, friends, part of our lives and we were such an integral part of theirs. We knew everything about them and their families. We had met their grandchildren and knew about their son's recent holiday or the family dog. We were connected. Then Covid tore through it, through us.

Outside of work, I try to be as social as possible and enjoy the life that I value. I go out with friends, spend time with family and try new activities. I adore seeing shows at the many, great theatres in the area. I tried kayaking the last year with the family and loved it, although it's not easy! I strive to get a good balance between resting and enjoying life, alongside working. We live in a lovely part of the world and I like to go out and about walking, soaking up the atmosphere – especially in the warmer weather.

Me and my children

I'm Walker born and bred and have lived in my street for over 30 years. My daughter lives next door to me so it's lovely to have her and my granddaughter, Ella, on my doorstep. It's always been home for me. Some people say bad things about the place but there is so much that is positive. Perhaps people aren't as sociable and friendly as they were in the past, maybe keeping themselves to themselves more these days but people still lend a hand. There is a community spirit and lots to get involved with. Pottery Bank Community Centre is an example of this. The centre means a lot to many people and I hope it continues to thrive.

Me with my children and grandchildren

Me with my daughter, Karen.

I have good support around me like I always have. My close friends Jacqui and Sheila have always been there for me. My kids are also amazing and supportive. They have all done well for themselves

175

and I'm extremely proud of them all, for their careers as well as their beautiful personalities. I have three grandchildren and love them dearly. I'm very blessed.

My hope for the future is that attitudes change towards our older communities and that more resources become available to support the ageing population. We have so little respect for elderly people as a society now. Older people living in poverty, loneliness, and ill-health. It saddens me and more needs done. We are all living longer and someday, that old person will be us.

Hazel Jones, aged 60
Dedicated to the strong women in my life; my little mam, Sheila Jones and her sister, my second Mam, Alice Bland.

A Place of Acceptance

I was born in a fishing port town called Lowestoft, Suffolk in the late 1940s. At the time, the town had somewhat of a small, village mentality. Perhaps not now, but in the 1950s there was a big focus on roles and expectations in society. Women behaved a certain way and men behaved a certain way and for many communities, that was that – deviation from the norm was not acceptable. The children at this time struggled with the era of parents' post-war traditions and the new decade and movement of the 1960s trickling in.

I was the eldest child in my family and my mother always wanted her firstborn to be a boy. As a result, I didn't have a good relationship with my mother. For the first few hours of my life, I was called Davida. My name was changed after people commented I couldn't be called that and I became Janet, which was a popular name at the time. As I got older, the rejection and resentment from my mother about my gender stuck with me. When I was a toddler, my parents had another child, this time a boy that my mother desperately wanted, David. My parents then went on to have a third child, another boy named Robert. Relationships with my mother were strained throughout my life and although I have tried to recall some good times and some positive memories with my mother, sadly I can't.

A class mate and me in the school yard

As a child, I played with cars and trains. I loved them and I still do. They were passed to my brother when he was born. I did have a few "feminine" toys and when I was given a Silver Cross pram, I actually turned it into a go-cart! Childhood was confusing and it made making sense of the world hard. There was a resentment harboured from my mother's own childhood that she inflicted on us, myself being the target in particular. But one lesson I did learn from my mother was to never treat my children the way I was treated.

My father was a very strong character, who worked hard selling paint in an ironmonger's. He worked for the same company all his life from the age of 14 years old until he retired. It's where he met my mother as she worked in the finance team. She was good with numbers and I remember times that we would be sat at home, round the table as a family. My mother would set us math's problems. It felt competitive and a way to highlight my and my father's weaknesses. My father and I were always on the same team, not answering quickly enough. It felt like another way to put me down. My mother died 26 years ago. We never made peace but in many ways, I still think she is around and have had a few strange encounters. I had a closer relationship with my father but there were issues with his attitude, like many people at that time. Father was old-fashioned. He wasn't accepting of different people and I always felt he held discriminatory views. However, towards the end of his life, I realised he had been "playing me," and in fact didn't hold such views.

Myself and my siblings all went to grammar school and my mother, being good with numbers, used to test us frequently and not just at the dining table. I was great at algebra, but struggled with some topics, being delighted if I got double figures in exams! I recall one of the teachers saying that they had another child with the surname Secret in the school but he couldn't possibly be related to me as he was so clever. However, I was good with words and spelling and I had a very creative imagination. Art has been a massive part of my life and I feel creativity has always been in my body, pumping through my veins alongside my blood. Creativity hasn't always been embraced and I feel in the past, people were often perceived in a negative light for having a creative drive and desire to express themselves and their personality through the arts. I passed some exams but grammar school wasn't a wonderful experience. I felt alone in many ways and didn't fit in visually. I had bright ginger hair and stood out, for perhaps the wrong reasons. I was bullied and as my personality developed, I found fitting in harder. At 14 years old, I was bullied so much at school that I was put on medication for my mental health that I ended up taking for 24 years before having a break from it.

My father

Me as a young child

In 1968 I got married at the age of 18 years old. I remember before getting married not feeling anything for my fiancé. My husband was my escape, but it was the wrong thing to do. I recall visiting my family doctor before the wedding, in a desperate attempt for some guidance and advice. The family doctor, who knew us all, understood but stated that my mother and I couldn't live together and I couldn't expect her to leave. My husband was ten years older than me and had much more life experience. I was still a child in many ways but felt I had little choice. It was a better option than staying at home, absorbing more resentment from my mother. My husband and I had nothing in common and I remember him telling me that if the nurse he had affection for who had moved to New Zealand came back, he would marry her. It was another relationship where I didn't feel good enough.

One positive from my first marriage, was my mother-in-law who was wonderful and we got on exceptionally well. My first husband and I had two children, Julien and Adrian, aged 54 and 52 years old. But our marriage was lacking in love, companionship, and common ground. We were married for seven years and during that time, I did meet other men. There were times I felt trapped and would go away for a few days, usually to France, which I first visited when I was 14 years old with school and fell in love with the place. Unhappiness in my marriage fuelled my poor mental health but the children kept me going much of the time, along with alcohol.

So many women in those days were in unhappy marriages and I'm sure many men were unhappy also. Divorce was frowned upon, seen as alien and there was the expectation that you got married, had kids, and became a housewife. Women's roles were different and we were expected to conform. It didn't mean all men were abusive or wrong, it was society, culture, and history dripping into the daily lives of families with little change on the horizon. Some women may have been happy with that, but I wasn't and I yearned for love, friendship, acceptance, and happiness. My mental health was poor throughout my marriage and I knew it would only get worse if I didn't change my life. I took an overdose when I was 24 years old and after surviving that, I became aware that it would only get worse and would likely happen again if I remained in my marriage. In those days, there wasn't as much help or understanding. I was medicated with limited support. I wanted to use art as part of my therapy but my husband would tell me I wasn't an artist and it was ridiculous thinking. It was drilled into me, cemented into my soul that I was a mother and should have been satisfied with my lot. However, the whisper in me became a voice, then a scream too loud to ignore.

I left my first husband when my oldest son, Julien was almost six years old and my husband kept the boys as punishment. I remember previously trying to get help from local charities. However, many were religious so advice was to work on my marriage. I knew I couldn't go back home, to my family, they had made that clear. There was no help. I ended up getting into a relationship with another man who was an artist and was physically abusive. We had a son together, Max. One morning I remember when Max was a few months old and he was lying in his cot beside our bed. Out of nowhere, my partner assaulted me, splitting my lip. I lay in bed, silent in shock as my mouth bled, tasting the iron tinge of fresh blood as it filled my mouth. The next morning, I took Max and walked to the local hospital to get my injury treated. I used the old excuse of 'I walked into a door.' It wasn't questioned and in that era, there was such limited understanding and support for people experiencing domestic abuse and it wasn't something that the police pursued. I had several stitches in my lip and mouth and still have the scar today.

By this point, I was still only 30 years old and felt that I had been bullied all my life. Always a target by someone, like an injured bird vulnerable to prey. However, reflecting now, all these experiences made me who I am. The positive experiences and the negatives shaped me and helped build the person I wanted to be, even though it often felt painful. I never gave up, even at times when I felt myself falling, the ground dissolving beneath me. I kept going, for my children. Things would be different in today's society if my life played out again. But even though my first two relationships were negative, I had my beautiful family and I'm eternally grateful for that.

I met my next partner when he came to study in the area. I had started college, studying O-Levels after not receiving many qualifications whilst at school. We got to know each other after I left my husband, Max's dad when Max was three years old. Planning began to move to Newcastle, where he had secured a place to study at Newcastle University and I was going to study at the Polytechnic. It was 1988 and I felt I had been gifted the golden ticket out of my home town to study in Newcastle. Before this time, I had never considered going to university as I never thought I was good enough. Society and my relationships with people, and subsequently my relationship with myself made me feel I could never succeed in studying. I had secured a qualification at college and wanted to learn more. I was a mature student but it was a chance I was certain I wouldn't get again and Max was young enough to settle in another town. Julien and Adrian were in their late teens at this time and had settled lives in Lowestoft.

I was 39 years old when we relocated to the North East. We needed to find somewhere to live, in a new town that was a long distance away from our current home. But I had to get out. The attitudes of people around me were negative, insular, and with a belief that felt completely out of sync with my own. Generations of people had performed the same jobs in the same industries, like many towns with their trade – in this case fishing. But I felt different. I was different and difference wasn't encouraged, accepted, or celebrated. I felt suffocated in my birth town. My creative wings were clipped and I would forever be in a cage. It wasn't just me, some of the townspeople didn't like anyone different. It's wrong to say every person in Lowestoft was like that, they weren't. However, many were and it was oppressive and suffocating. Newcastle promised fresh air.

However, a few weeks before we were due to begin a new life in Newcastle, my partner decided he no longer wanted to be with me. He told me I would be better off staying in Lowestoft where I knew people. I had been trapped in this town for so long, I was almost out and I couldn't stop now, not when I could see the finish line. I told him I was going, after securing my place at the local Poly to study library and information studies. The day I came to Newcastle, I drove up from Lowestoft. I had never driven more than 40 miles, and I had to drive over 300 miles to get here. I remember stopping at the service station on the way and sitting there for two hours, wondering how I could do it. But I started the engine again, determination fuelling me and made the rest of the journey to start my new life with Max.

It took me until I was 39 years old to get the confidence and courage to leave and embark on a life where just perhaps I could be my true self and be accepted. There was something about Newcastle that immediately felt like home, like the cosiest of dressing gowns enveloping me. There were many different people from diverse backgrounds. Friendly people who were welcoming, kind, and non-judgmental. In addition to this, Newcastle had and still does have a real culture around arts and creativity. People could express themselves through art without being ostracised. People could simply be themselves and although no city is perfect and there will always be problematic people, it felt like another world in Newcastle and a world I wanted to live in!

I moved into a house in Newcastle, taking in a lodger to help with bills. My partner soon travelled up with more belongings and ended up staying for around four years. He also attended university in Newcastle. It was a challenge for us both studying with a family, sharing childcare and a computer. We got by and I really enjoyed my studies. Lots of things changed when I lived in Newcastle, including me becoming vegetarian. I also felt I began, perhaps for the first time in my life, finding myself and being able to be myself. I met new people in a city that felt like a whole new world in many ways. I finished my degree, obtaining a 2:1. After years of not feeling I had achieved, I was proud of myself. I felt like a child being able to cycle without stabilises at last! A child who was in her early 40s.

I soon discovered I was pregnant with my fourth child, Molly. When I was about seven months pregnant, my partner left us. He stayed in Newcastle but our relationship ended. In all of my relationships, I have struggled to find healthy and happy love. Incompatible people, abuse, lack of support – it has all played a role. I'm not perfect, I've made mistakes myself but I'm from a generation where it was so hard to leave and women were treated with contempt by many. Life of course has changed now and I'm so happy for the future women and men also. Molly has a great relationship with her father and I always felt that even if parents don't get on, the children should not suffer and should always see their parents, as long as it's safe.

After studying and when the children were at school, I wanted to work. I had always struggled with my own mental health and as a 14-year-old, I was initially diagnosed with bipolar. I was on mental health medication for a large part of my adolescent and adult life. I received a small amount of counselling and support from a community mental health nurse when Molly was young. However, after being discharged from psychiatry, the community mental health service ended. After my own experiences, I had an understanding and empathy towards people who battled with their emotional and mental well-being. It seemed natural for me to want to work in the field. I had never received the right support myself but I wanted to help others, help ease their painful load.

A neighbour at the time mentioned a local charity supporting people in the community to manage their mental health so I explored the service and found a local vacancy. I applied and was successful, subsequently joining the team. It was challenging work, but rewarding. The people accessing the service each day had many complexities and the service supported a variety of individuals. I did enjoy the role, with mostly nice colleagues on the team and hope I made a difference to people. In lots of ways it also helped me and my well-being. However, after about 12 years and struggling with my own mental health, I lost my job.

Newcastle was home from day one and I have friends here that I first made when I arrived in the city. Friends who have healed me in many ways and brought out the shine that was always dimmed in me. I hope I also bring something to their lives.

My friend and me at a Women's History Month event (2023)

There are small things I miss from Lowestoft including the menacing melody sound of thunderstorms that never seem to match here in Newcastle. Things that are the same are the sounds of helicopters, trains, and squawking seagulls. My mental health still fluctuates but my doctor is good so I am hoping to get some more support. I feel lonely at times but attend a local service for older people and I like to get involved with arts locally. I also have carers twice daily as I have had diabetes for 40 years. I have type one brittle diabetes and it has been very challenging. I have been in a diabetic coma before so need to monitor my health closely. The carers are lovely people and keep me well, checking up on me daily.

Me in my home

It can be difficult to get out myself, however, to be able to walk out dressed as I dress, being who I am, smiling at people and receiving a smile back makes Newcastle my heart and soul home. Not having to apologise for who I am and how I live is peace for my mind. Acceptance is one of the most important things in the world and I never take it for granted.

Jan Secret, aged 73.

A Care Calling

It was the mid-1950s when I was born and we lived in a two-bedroomed, downstairs flat on Janet Street in Byker. With an older sister and older brother, I was the third and youngest child. Mam brought us up on her own and in those days it was challenging for single parents, not only financially but also due to stigma and gender expectations at the time. Challenges which sadly still exist today.

Home was happy enough, even with our outside toilet that stood, along with our coal house in our back yard. Mam would go to the wash house, on Shipley Street, each Monday. I remember she made a trolley from a basket, that we used to get our fruit and vegetables in. She nailed wheels to the basket and attached a walking stick as a handle, to help her transport the washing. She would return and the washing would be hung out on the back lane, along with everyone else's. Nothing was easy in those days, no quick buys for convenience from online shopping. People modified items to make life a little less difficult. Alongside the weekly trip to the wash house, we had a poss tub in the house and a mangle in the back yard for items needing washing in between the week. The things you only see in pictures now.

Mam (right)

We had a tin bath hanging outside in the back yard. When it was bath day, we all had to wait our turn. As I was the youngest, I was last in the queue and by the time Mam, my brother, George, and my sister, Maureen, had been in the bath there would be rings of scum marks that accompanied the water. George is three years older than me and still alive. Maureen was two years older and has sadly now passed. They were really close and I was a bit of the black sheep, a little bit of a rebel.

When I was young you knew everyone in the street, by their name. If they spent a lot of time with the family, they would be called "Auntie," or "Uncle." We wouldn't dare do anything naughty as it would get back to Mam. We had respect for our elders and especially the police. Crime wasn't like it is now with all the knife crime and cybercrime. It was safer and felt safer – the community looked out for one another. The world is a dangerous place now. The justice system doesn't help and people commit crimes and get away with it, or a lenient sentence. There is no deterrent and criminals are getting younger. Perhaps it starts with teaching in schools and even if this helps one person, it makes a difference. However, some things have improved such as the establishment of food banks and financial help. If you had no food in the past, you would have to beg but now you can get some help.

Me as a toddler

As a youngster, I went to St Vincent's school and I loved it. It was also where Mam worked, as a dinner lady. My father wasn't on the scene, so Mam did everything alone, us helping where we could. I remember food would be things like homemade soup, stews, and mince and dumplings. All home-cooked, nutritious food. Mam would make rice pudding with cinnamon and eating was family time, all of us together. Outside of school I played on the streets and would be in my element. We'd play two balls, football, chase, French skipping, anything we could think of. No distractions, just friends playing and laughing.

I remember when we were little wearing plastic shoes that were bought from Woolworths. We had a brown pair for school and a white pair for church. As our feet grew, Mam used to cut the back off so they transformed into flip-flops. Then when our feet grew again, she would cut off the front so our toe could pop out the front like the first daffodils of spring, but a lot less pretty to look at! They were like what we would call sliders now. Perhaps we were the pioneers of foot fashion, all those years ago, but it was horrendous for us at the time. Even more so when I wanted to join the Brownies and they wouldn't let me sign up as you had to wear proper shoes and I only had plastic ones. When I eventually got a pair of leather shoes, Mam put segs on the bottom to make them last longer. I would clip clop along making noises like a tap dancer.

Me at school

In senior school, I was less studious and was a bit of a class clown. I used to get 'must try harder,' and 'talks too much,' on my school reports. I changed my mind each week about what I wanted to do with my life. After leaving school, my first job was working at a ticket shop, Blundells in Newcastle. It was a seasonal job for Christmas, in the toy department. I wasn't kept on after Christmas but I worked briefly in Nazareth House in Newcastle, which was an orphanage for children. I subsequently secured a job in Kingston upon Thames, working in a home supporting disabled children. It was at

Teddington Lock and was very close to the ITV Studios, which meant we had many famous visitors to see the children. I was around 17 or 18 years old and thought it would be the making of me. Thinking back, it was big responsibility moving away from the North East, alone and to a job with adult demands.

Me as a teenager

Despite enjoying my job in London, I soon got home sick. People didn't say hello on the streets, like they did in Newcastle. I didn't have real friends and despite meeting my husband there, I was away from my family and the community familiar to me. My comfort blanket had been removed and it was a culture shock being in a new city. It became overwhelming so I returned to the North East. My then partner came up north with me and we eventually got married.

In London I had found my passion to work in the care field. I wanted to continue a career helping people so I applied to the local hospitals for a place on a nurse training course and was successful. It felt like nursing could be a perfect career for me and I patiently waited until February 1976 to start my training, excited like a kid waiting for their birthday. I had always worked since leaving school, so took a job working in a kitchen near the ship yards, pan scrubbing for a few months until the course commenced. Eventually, the training began and I loved it, studying then securing work as a nurse.

My children when they were young

I had continued working when I had my three children; David, Stephen, and Kristine. When Kristine was two years old, my husband and I separated. It was on good terms and the children kept seeing their father, alongside us sharing a car and a dog. At this point, it was the late 1980s and I was then practising as a district nurse. I really enjoyed the job and felt I was helping people in need. I met some characters over the years, some it was very challenging and watching people in pain and suffering was very difficult. Many go into the care profession to make a difference but cases don't always go the way we want them to, no matter how much we hope. There wasn't a massive deal of support back in those days and deaths and illness took its toll eventually and I left the profession with a heavy heart.

I then tried working in nursing homes as a nurse, but it wasn't for me. It was nice being part of a team and around other workers, this was something I hadn't experienced as a district nurse, working solo. However, it was hard work and the services were always short-staffed. It put pressure on everyone on shift who had to be so many things to so many people in need, it could feel suffocating. It was exhausting but I hope I made a difference to some people. Although I was nursing, it was alongside carers which is such a hard job and paid poorly. In roles like that, you simply have to employ the right people, which can be difficult when incentives are limited.

In between jobs and sometimes alongside jobs, I worked in the pubs on Shields Road, in Byker. I worked in almost all the pubs and had friends in the trade. There were some wild times and I met so many colourful characters, all with a tale to tell! I always had to work, the kids constantly needed something or other but luckily, I enjoyed most of the jobs I had.

My last role before retirement was working locally within the mental health field. I worked in the same role for almost 20 years and enjoyed this work, supporting people who struggled to manage their mental health and assisting with all elements of their lives. At times it was heavy going and heart-breaking but it was also lovely to see people learning how to manage their mental health and rebuild their confidence, like a jigsaw coming together. It's always felt natural to me to work with people and try to help them in their hours of need. If I could assist them to make their lives a little bit more positive it was all worth it. The simple things sometimes resulted in the biggest impact.

I only retired last year and I have been busier than ever. I don't know where I got the time to go to work all those years! I attend Pottery Bank Community Centre, with my daughter, Kristine and friend, Linda. There always seems to be something going on and I have learnt so much, developing my skills such as sewing, cooking, and crafts. Pottery Bank is the perfect place to meet people, try new things, and get involved with the community. My days are full and I'm pleased to be occupied and around people. Work was such a massive part of my life, I knew I couldn't just stop when I retired and do nothing.

My daughter, Kristine, me
and my friend, Linda

Me, enjoying retirement

I know some of the people where I live now but it's not like it used to be. When I was younger we would all sit on our doorsteps and chat. People knew one another and showed interest. That doesn't happen now. There isn't the closeness that we had in the past. Perhaps people are just too busy, or frightened. Perhaps people lack trust or are more out for themselves. It's a shame, but I still love the area and I have a lifetime of memories from Byker.

Christine Allen, aged 67.

Dedicated to my sister Maureen and my brother George.

Community Heart

I was born in Lincoln before my family moved to Newcastle when I was around three years old. My parents, two older brothers, and me settled in Westerhope. Here, I went to school, before we moved to Hazelrigg when I attended high school at Seaton Burn. I remember at school being desperate to learn to type and when we lived in Westerhope, our neighbour taught me how to. I recall learning the skill on her beautiful, old typewriter when I was around 10 years old. I thought I was the bees-knees pressing those magical keys and seeing the letters appear on the paper! It started my love for typing and I soon received a typewriter for Christmas. I knew it would be the career for me and I went on to study typing at school.

At the time of exams, it was a choice of metal keyed, manual typewriter or an electronic typewriter. I passed my exams then I started working through what at the time was a YTS (Young Training Scheme) and learnt how to use a computer. Of course, it was a lot easier and smoother, but there was something about the typewriter that had a charm, a panache that no computer could encapsulate. The noise of the typewriter, although took a lot of getting used to, was something that I had grown to love and the computer created a different tune of tapping music that took time to get into the beat.

When I was 16 years old computers started to grow in popularity, taking the place of the typewriter. During my YTS I learnt more about the changing technology, alongside general office work and secretarial duties. Within the course, I attended a few work placements. One was at a builder's merchant in Walker, which I hated and only stayed for a few weeks. At the time, the male staff were all very sexist and it was an awful environment. This was in the late 1980s and after some time, I left the YTS after completing my exams and worked at a local supermarket whilst looking for employment in the admin and secretarial field.

I soon found a job with a local company that went into receivership a few years later. One of the directors subsequently set up his own business and offered me a job, which I gratefully accepted. It was a design company and my role was all admin, dealing with enquiries and reception. I trained in graphic design through the company, which led to more studies including computing.

A few years later I started my own family and then when it was time to return to work, I began a role in a sports club on reception that fitted around the children. In 2002, I secured a job in Walker at NCH, which is now Action for Children. In those days it was called St Anthony's Children's House, known locally as "The Children's House." The role was admin support and Action for Children was based at Pottery Bank so I became familiar with the centre and area. It was a charity and in 2012-13 funding changed resulting in some staff moving out to other locations and roles. A few of us were left in the centre, including myself. I was part-time during this period and I was asked to cover reception by the community centre. It became a dual role for a while until funding changed again with Action for Children and I was due to work in a different location. At this point, Pottery Bank offered me a job, which I accepted.

I began my role as a centre coordinator at Pottery Bank in 2014. I attended management training and progressed to centre manager. I already knew many of the locals and in my role, I began to meet more residents. Some of the people I met with Action for Children as children, were now adults bringing their own children into the centre, which was wonderful to see. That's one of the special things about Pottery Bank – it's generational. We have had three and four generations of families in here, each with their own stories of Walker and Byker and for the youngsters, a lifetime of memory-making and stories to come. It's magical to witness and I'm grateful that I can be part of such an important community resource.

Walker has changed significantly since I first began working here over two decades ago. Streets were demolished; houses and schools gone, services closed and new ones opened. The area used to have a bad reputation and it was reinforced by people who didn't live in the area. However, it feels much more positive now. Of course, there are issues like there are in every town and society but most people feel happy, safe, and part of the community. I remember when I worked for Action for Children and someone broke into the office, stealing staff's car keys and subsequently their cars! I'm pleased to say that hasn't happened again. But things have changed, perhaps people grow up and see they don't want negative situations for their kids. Crime exists, like it does everywhere but trends in criminal behaviours have changed focus.

The Pottery Bank Community Centre has also changed over the years. Previously, the site used to be a care home with a day centre attached. The care home was demolished and the day centre function remained, which at the time was called the Thomas Gaughan Centre. The community centre changed focus to try and be more for the community as a whole, rather than older people in 1995. The centre continued to develop and people of all ages visited so funding became available for activities and groups. The aim was to make the centre accessible for all, inclusive, and a place to learn, have fun, and meet new people. In 2012 the local council granted us money to refurbish the centre. The refurb took around four months and once completed, we decided to change the name of the centre to Pottery Bank Community Centre (after the place we are based, Pottery Bank).

We then decided our charity should become a limited company and have a board of directors, opening the doors to potential support from grants to keep our services going and developing, always evolving like the community around us. The Pottery Bank Community Centre logo was designed by children at a local school and we recruited local, female residents to our board of directors.

Centre renaming day

We analysed what groups, activities and learning had been available over the years to ensure we were meeting the needs of the local people. After exploring funding streams we secured some money to work with the women of Walker around seven years ago. This involved supporting local women who had children and may have struggled to participate in activities or attend courses due to a lack of childcare. We began offering groups with childcare on-site. We organised a range of courses and skill-building sessions for local women to learn and develop, as well as focus on employability, connecting with new people, and building confidence. Cooking, food hygiene certificates, hair and beauty, first aid, health and social care courses were all included. Some of the women then went on to volunteer in places, secure employment, or go on to further education. It isn't always about obtaining the ideal job and full-time work, it's about bringing people together and learning, gaining experience, making new friends, and knowing how to access resources. The women loved the sessions then we expanded them to teach children cooking through our Kid's Café project. Here, children learnt about healthy eating, preparing food, what ingredients and utensils to use, and exploring taste. Alongside this, we would run healthy activities such as exercise and crafts. These were offered after school and in school holidays. At the end of the classes, the children would set a menu, delivering a meal with full service for family and friends. This was facilitated through our own, on-site catering company, Community Catering Initiative Limited and the staff, Laura and Pam. The community thrived and we still deliver similar projects today.

With the nature of charities, funding constantly changes and we have always had a cycle of funding ending, eagerly awaiting the outcome of bids for more support, then delivering new projects. It's hard and unpredictable but essential that we have resources for the community and the residents who now rely on the centre for so many reasons. Pottery Bank has become the community's heart and it must keep beating. The pandemic had a monumental impact on the centre, alongside the community and now we are dealing with the energy crisis and cost of living impact. We do a lot of consultations with residents and co-produce services. Currently, we are trying to focus on the basics that people need to manage daily and weekly living, to survive and manage the catastrophic impact of poverty. We have our internet café, a budgeting and benefits drop-in, as well as providing a warm space at the centre – which means people can come in over the winter and get a warm drink and a sandwich each day for free.

Activity wise we deliver an exercise group, a weekly health check session, cooking lessons and take-home family cooking, as well as a writing group. We offer a weekly food hub which is a pay-as-you-feel model allowing people to contribute the money they can afford for a bag of food, donated from local supermarkets and FareShare. The money people donate for their shopping is collected and each month this is used to purchase essential cleaning and toiletry products that go back into the offer. Once a month, people receive a bag of these items as part of their shop. We top these items up with small pots of grants we receive to ensure people have essential items. The lack of this resource would have a significant, detrimental impact on our residents.

Cheque from the National Lottery Community Fund, 2019

The Food Hub began during lockdown after a local café, Magic Hat Café had surplus food to donate to the community. Laura and Pam from Catering Company, and Hayley who works on reception and as a domestic, along with our local volunteers, offered to help and the centre was able to create food parcels for people in need. We were also able to make cooked meals for people to collect. It kept the community smiling and gave them a little something to look forward to – those things mattered so much during that time, a glimmer of light during such a dark period. Additionally, we have a clothing bank, allowing people to get good quality, second-hand clothing and in school holidays, we provide activities for the full family.

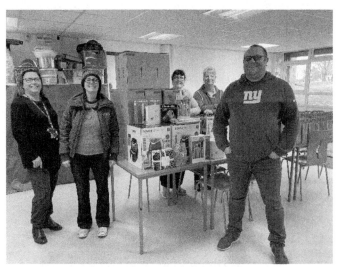

Food Hub with donations from Sainsbury's, 2023

On-site at Pottery Bank, there is an allotment and garden that was used during lockdown. Courses and gardening volunteering is offered. Last year we started a men's potter shed group and around 10 men began attending, many of which hadn't interacted or spoken to someone for days and weeks. The group became a sanctuary and a place where men could talk. This still runs and new friendships have been made, skills learnt and plenty of produce grown! It's now open to all but the men still meet, which is lovely and exactly what we wanted. Friendships that continue after a course ends is one of the many legacies we hope materialises from our services.

Me outside of the Community Allotment
(Sign designed by local children) 2016

Community Allotment build, 2013

Pottery Bank work with local community groups & services that provide childcare and additional services for the community and we refer people to an array of services and support across the area. We will always listen to what people want and strive to deliver something that works for the community. Sometimes this is about working with partner agencies, supporting one another. All helping for the benefit of the community, the way it should be.

Walker over the years has changed dramatically, in my opinion and definitely for the better. Visually, the demolition of places, full streets in many cases has led to re-development. The regeneration of the area brought new services, money, and amenities. It's one of the most disadvantaged towns in the North East and has a stigma, but people living here don't see it like that. It's their home, they love it and help one another. It's rich with community and support and that's priceless.

I didn't personally grow up in Walker, but I grew into the job here and it feels like home in so many ways. I've been here for over two decades and can't imagine working anywhere else. I feel like I fit in and the community are so nice, welcoming, and grateful. Walker and Byker are wonderful communities. The centre feels like a home from home for local people and every day it's lovely to work in an environment that creates an impact, opportunities and connections. Friendships made, skills developed, services offered – it's all needed in any community and especially in a community that has struggled over the years and still does. The staff at Pottery Bank make the centre what it is. They work with all their heart, and the dedication and kindness they show each day make a massive difference. It's more than a job to everyone, it runs through them, part of their lives. They love Walker and they love what they do and I hope we can continue being here in the heart of the community for many years to come.

Jacqui Higgins, aged 52.

Poems and prose by story holders

Avoid The North

Don't move there, drop your daft ideas.

They won't accept you, they'll confirm your fears.

You talk posh, you're southern, you're not like
them,

So you'll be alone, rejected, they'll make you gan
hyem.

People say that though wherever you move,

Lancashire, Yorkshire or Wales and I proved.

It's a southern perspective, you'll be out on your
ass,

That you can't fit in northern when your vowels
don't pass.

We moved to Newcastle, took a risk, dared to dare,

Found welcoming people, found people who care.

Hearts worn on sleeves, no respectable hiding,

If you wear your heart too, you'll find lives
coinciding.

Seven bridges in minutes, that view won't get old,

Pass Angel, pass Tyne, don't wrap up in the cold.

Nah, that's a lie too cos the Geordies aren't
thickies,
But we'd seen only drunks, crime and seventies
brickies.
There's a god of the river, a precious community,
Poverty means there's scarce opportunity.
Northerners create it themselves, well some of us
do,
Overcome finance inequality, make Newcastle new.
I sit here today, poorest part of the city,
Look down to the river, aye the north is dead
pretty.
I'm blessed that we moved here, I don't want to
leave,
I'm one of them now, with my heart on my sleeve.

Clare Matthews

Grounded

I open the back door,

A cool breeze on my face.

6.30 am nobody about.

The dew on the grass,

It wets my slippers,

As I walk over the lush lawn.

I approach my tree and say,

'Hello old friend.'

Leaning my face against the bark,

As I put my arms around,

My silver birch tree.

It feels solid,

Roots in the ground,

The bark I tell all my troubles too.

It feels like hugging a familiar friend,

That would never let me down.

That special place on my tree,

Where my hand fits like a glove.

The leaves flutter in the wind,

Just as the sun is rising.

It fills my heart with joy,

It settles my mind,

And helps me face the day.

Pauline Sheldon

Nothing's changed

Nothing's changed.

I'm still me.

I like the same things as before.

I drink wine and watch TV.

Nothing's changed.

I go to work.

I see my friends.

I dance a little.

Nothing's changed.

I wear the same clothes,

(Except maybe for certain tops),

And definitely not a swimsuit!

Nothing's changed.

You don't need to worry about me.

I feel fine about myself.

I always bolt the bathroom door.

Chris

Laura's Story

In 1992, my daughter, Ashley, joined the playgroup at St. Anthony's Children's House. My other two children were at primary school, so I had time on my hands and I started to stay for a cup of coffee there, at the drop-in. I never used to go out, only to my mam's during the day and I had no real confidence. From sitting in the drop-in, I joined the project support committee and was able to take up my studies again through tutors who visited the family centre. As a result, I was able to take my exams in English and maths, achieving a distinction – something I'd never been able to do at school as I had missed a lot of schooling due to illness.

In 2003, I became a project worker at the Children's House. My role was mainly working with the older children in the out-of-school groups. This again, helped boost my confidence and I was able to use this confidence to support and encourage the local young people in the groups.

One of my biggest confidence boosters was abseiling from the Copthorne Hotel to fundraise for NCH and I was also asked to talk at other NCH functions, such as the opening of their Newcastle office, about my experiences. My children also became more confident by attending playgroups and after-school groups. In later life, my son secured his first job through people I had met via NCH.

I began volunteering at my local Methodist church youth club and then on the community centre management committee. I now run my own catering business with a friend (Community Catering) based in Pottery Bank Community Centre. My colleague was also a parent from the Children's House and we have been our own boss for many years now. Within the business, we include cookery lessons for adults and children and marginalised groups. We also had the opportunity to meet Jamie Oliver several years ago through our work. Additionally, we had the chance to travel to Italy and Germany to liaise with different communities and social enterprises.

So this is me now, a confident, outgoing person who enjoys her work in the community as a joint manager of Community Catering. But without NCH and the support of the Children's House, I would never have had these opportunities to develop myself or benefit my community and the children and families that live here.

Laura Forster

The Conversation

Being on Universal Credit is certainly no farce,

'Are you having a laugh!' my young teenage

daughter turned to me and said,

Whilst taking off her scarf.

'You've got it all to come.' I said, and she replied,

'Please don't say that, mum!

Whilst continuing to walk from the front door to

the kitchen, chewing her gum.

'Would you like a cup of tea? she said,

Before I sat down on the settee.

To which I replied, 'No, not right now for me.'

But, yet, what I would like you to see,

Is that nothing in this life is for free,

Not even the cup of tea that you kindly offered to

me.

In fact, the cost of living these days,

Is so high that it often makes me want to cry.

But I'm worried that even if I tried, my tears would touch the sky.

'Oh, come on, surely Mum, being on Universal Credit sounds like such fun.

Because I've seen so many claimants,

Spend time in the sun.'

'No, no,' I replied, that may well have been in the past,

Because nowadays the system,

Is a lot more daft!

'Oh my golly gosh, Mum,' she replied,

'In that case it seems, that I may well have to mask,

My fears for the task.'

'Of having to claim Universal Credit,

myself one day, because it sounds like it could be so vast!

And that being happy on it won't last!'

At this point, I gasped.

Because I then realized that we had just embarked,

Upon a whole new conversation that would need to

take place later on that day, and preferably after

dark!

Evette Callendar

Remembering

I close my eyes,

And there you are,

Attached, secure,

Content to nuzzle and to suckle.

It's strange,

The way I can still feel the sensation.

So totally connected,

just you and me.

Your tiny hand,

Resting on my breast.

Your fingers moving up and down,

In time with the rhythm of your sucking.

Mixed feelings:

I'm happy that nothing can erase so vivid a

memory.

I'm sad when I look down now,

At where my breast should be.

I'm glad it was there for you.

Chris

I Will Not Run Away

Why is it so perspiringly difficult,

To listen to people who tell you, you can?

They see you,

Watch you.

Say you should have confidence in you,

Because they do.

Three lightning bolts spoke to me,

Shared their belief, that I am able,

To write, to lead, to create, to inspire.

To flow with words, in sentences longer than these.

I trust. I respect them. And I want to run away.

Give me no responsibility,

I'm nothing. Don't matter.

I could never matter.

I'm the empty freak who cannot.

I'm doomed. Meaningless waste.

I cannot,

My head says it,

Comic Sans words on a cartoon screen.

You wascally wabbit.

You're an Acme confidence thief.

You'll realise, after three hilarious seconds,

You stepped off the cliff edge.

You will fall, fool, faker, fraud,

Be found out as you crash into the desert.

You'll never amount to nuffing.

You can't even spell or properly grammar,

And your story is not worth telling.

But she said, wow, it's important, going in the book.

And you can, brilliantly.

You can, do more.

Get your work out there,

It will bring healing and hope,

It will grant laughter and strength.

And she said.

We can do it together,

Light up the East End,

New consciousness above our poverty.

And she said, you'll be ace.

We've seen.

Heard the comments.

And we'll do more, let's create artistic wildfires.

Three She's in three days.

She's experienced.

She's creators.

She's fuse lighters.

She's who experienced me.

I will not run away.

I will not flee my potential, though blind to its

entirety.

Adventurously living.

Live adventurously, it's the Quakerly thing to do.

I will embrace the surprises,

Rise bravely.

Just with my voices,

Listen to the three Tyne goddesses, as they

prophesy my fate.

Listen,

Act,

Learn self-faith.

And I will fuck up, sometimes.

Tits up on thin ice, sometimes.

But success and scars are both weapons,

I will not run away.

I will not run away.

Fear cracks my bones, stalks the corridors.

Even when all goddesses fall silent,

I will run towards the promise.

I will not run away.

Clare Matthews

Bonfire Night

Bonfire Night,

Excitement in the air.

Days,

Weeks,

Months,

Guarding the wood.

Lord of the Flies,

In the dark back lanes.

Patrolling the walls,

Watching and waiting.

Night- time,

Bonfire Night,

Sparks flying,

Flames shooting.

Everyone, in our back lane,

Sitting together.

Snatched kisses behind the old wardrobes.

We throw potatoes into the fire,

Burnt black,

Cut open,

Butter dribbling.

Then eat the skins,

The heavenly smell.

Fire dies down,

Old chairs, old wardrobes,

Gone.

The bric -a -brac of life,

Gone.

They turn and leave,

On their way home, satisfied,

'Ta-ra.'

Until next year,

And we all start again.

Pauline Sheldon

Kid's Christmas Party

'Twas the night before Christmas, and down at the
club,

The kids were all dancing, and eating the grub.

There's Emily, Leanne, two of the girls,

Then Carly and Candice, doing their twirls.

In the corner, there's Connor, one of the boys,

Leonard's at the far side, making a noise.

The lads are not dancing, they're flirting instead,

The non-alcoholic punch, going to their head.

Connor's more popular, thinks he's the bee's knees,

'Coz the girls flock around him, in two's and three's.

Steven, he's cute and so is his brother,

But they're the kind of lads the girls want to
mother.

Luke is polite, he always says please,

There he is asking, 'Any more cheese?'

All different kids and when one of them smile,

That's when it makes our jobs worth-while.

The clock strikes half five, end of the day,

But they all want to stay.

Come back next year, we'll have a review,

But for now it's home for all of you.

They trudge out the door, not even a fight,

We wish them Merry Christmas,

And to all, a good night.

Laura Forster

H'yer we gan again!

Uh oh! H'yer we gan again! I'm in the middle of a beautiful warm shower and all of a sudden...I scream! I scream because the shower water has gone cold and I suspect that the gas has run out, yet again.

I scream, not out of terror, but out of fear. Fear because I wonder where I'm gonna get the next penny from to deal with this emergency.

The emergency is that, not only do I need to finish showering, but it is also a freezing cold day.

My house is dark, gloomy and freezing cold and I have two children to also shower and keep warm. But yet, upon inspection of my gas meter (after getting out of the shower, with now freezing cold droplets of water dripping off my body and onto the floor), it sharp becomes apparent to me that we have definitely run out of gas.

I then wrap a towel around me in a desperate attempt to keep warm.

Owww, howay man! How can this be? I say to myself, when I only topped up the gas

meter with credit just two days before? And how long is this going to go on for? I'm on

Universal Credit, which means I have a limited amount of income as it is.

Besides, when I used to credit my gas meter with the same amount of money a year

ago, it used to go so much further, but now it feels as if I'm having to top up the meter

with credit every single day! Especially since the prices have gone up.

This can't go on. Things need to change.

Now faced with the challenge of having to find money to credit my gas meter yet again,

I take a deep breath... put my hands on my hips... roll back my eyes, and sigh...

'H'yer we gan again!

Evette Callendar

Fish, Scraps, And Schizophrenia

I am the child of boil in the bag fish,

Of racist name biscuits, of ice cream with "stuff."

I am the child of new year fireworks in the

seventies,

Of scraps saved for chickens, of the cricket wicket

tree.

And when I was God in Queen's Square,

I desperately wanted to kiss the narrator.

She had brown eyes. She was even quieter than

me.

I did not kiss the narrator.

I am the product of things I want to forget,

Or want to remember.

A jumble sale rag life, shirt collars,

Jumbo jet wings from another age.

I played dictionary games, granddad taught me

logic,

I couldn't use scissors, catch stool balls or dance.

I got told off for reading books they said were too

advanced.

Jaws was confiscated and I was child confused,

Because the first man ever to see me, apart from dad,

Was Robert Shaw's brother so he almost killed that shark.

And the next man won the FA Cup the year before I was born.

He was on my wall when I was six,

When I believed liking football was the law.

I was the child who cried too much,

Until tears became silent.

Silent.

Silent.

I will not talk for you.

I was the child who sat for an entire day calculating,

The square root of three to thirty decimal places.

I was the child who grand-mastered Swingball,

Only when I played it against myself,

Which was almost always.

I was the child who astral projected,

Chatted with gods and devils in the bedroom,

And learned to balance chakras in the White Lodge.

I am the child diagnosed schizophrenic,

Then everything else psychiatric.

The child of a thousand inner voices,

The child who never quite belonged,

Strait jacketed even when naked in the road.

I am the child of boil in the bag fish,

But then I went vegetarian,

Even though I didn't like any vegetables.

I am the child of textured vegetable protein,

And that's not a childhood to be endured.

Clare Matthews

Me

I am a woman in every way,

Take each and everything, day by day.

Sometimes I laugh, sometimes I cry,

And half of the time I think,

Why, oh why, oh why?

Please don't cry.

Look up, look down, look all around.

Go forward, go forward, go forward bound.

Like it or lump it, is what I say,

Just get lost and on your way!

Jane

The Club

Mary looked in the mirror, she was very pleased with what she saw - hair done, red polka dot dress, high heels. She had been asked out by John, their first proper date. The Westbourne Club in Walker, sweet 16, although she looked 18 so she knew there would be no problem getting signed in.

John picked her up, he looked handsome, she was thrilled, excitement rising as she looked forward to her first date, at The Club. It was packed! They went to sit down, a woman with a beehive and a sparkly dress said

'Hey, that seat is taken!'

No argument, no explanation. They looked around the room, embarrassed, spotted John's family and hurried over to sit with them.

The band, the comedian, the compare, the noise – everyone having the time of their lives. Mary was mesmerised by it all and felt so grown up as if she had finally arrived.

Then suddenly it all stopped, the house lights went up, the compare walked up to the microphone and shouted,

'Time for bingo.'

The spell had been broken.

John stood up, looked at Mary and said,

'We, (he meant the men) are going to the Men's Bar for a pint. You (meaning her) stay here with these', he said pointing at the women, 'and play bingo.'

Mary, temper rising, stood up and said loudly,

'This is supposed to be a date, I'm going home.'

Out of the corner of her eye she looked at them, they looked back, shocked. She left The Club, laughed all the way home and thought *Never again*.

Pauline Sheldon

The Danger of Drugs

Eleven and twelve,

A caring lad.

Then turned fifteen,

And he went bad.

No more kisses,

No more hugs.

He's found a substance,

He's found drugs.

Didn't care or think,

He didn't feel.

All he wanted,

Was his fiver deal.

I thought that things,

Couldn't get worse.

Then he starting stealing,

From my purse.

Ten o' clock,

He should've been in bed.

But he was out on the streets,

With his mates, instead.

When he came home,

He's was off his head.

I knew in my heart,

He'd end up dead.

I sit and think,

What could have been.

If he had only lived,

Past seventeen.

I only had him,

For a while.

But every day,

I miss his smile.

He was my life,

My world, my joy.

But now I've lost,

My darling boy.

No more loud music,

No more sport.

Coz his young life,

Has been cut short.

I never really knew,

The true danger.

Until my own son,

Was a total stranger.

So mums all over,

Please be aware.

Of the serious risks,

Of drugs out there.

Teach your kids,

The danger of drugs.

And you won't miss out,

On the kisses and hugs.

Look for the signs,

They try to hide.

Weight loss, munchies,

Their eyes open wide.

I wish I'd know more,

When my son was at home.

But now he's in heaven,

And I'm all alone.

Laura Forster

Wobbly Tooth

I remember the sensation: the journey of the wobbly tooth – just a fact of childhood.

Slight movement, the first stage in the disconnect. Then, so loose! I could poke my tongue right in behind it – swivel it.

For days it dangled from the finest of threads – no longer fit for purpose but not quite ready to make the final break.

And then, it's gone. Connection broken. **Was it ever really there?**

I remembered all this one day when my heart broke.

You see, I'd thought it was already broken beyond repair; that I was living with the stone-weight of pain and loss that now defined me.

I honestly thought that there was nothing left to break............

And then, the severing of a thread I hadn't known existed.

Terrifying emptiness.

Chris

Pitch & Toss

Old men with big ears,

And cloth caps, gather round.

Pitch & toss for money,

Lookout in place,

The chat, the club,

No women, no children allowed.

Everybody in their proper place,

Including the police.

Dark street, corner shops,

Little lights twinkling.

Old women with weighing machines, sweet and
sugar,

Making a bob or two.

Kids playing rounders on a summer night,

Knocky-nine door,

Hiding round corners – giggling.

Mothers calling kids in.

The women gathering in the back lane,

Warm barmy nights, open back doors.

Sitting in their makeshift chairs,

A problem shared.

Just make sure your net curtains are clean.

Pauline Sheldon

Proud

Today I am proud,

Of being a woman, becoming free, life as
conqueror.

Of remaining true when accused of falsehood.

Of getting all the washing up done and put away,

And laundry on the day I reached my last pair of
knickers.

Today I am proud,

Of standing without crawling on my knees.

Of quiet speech, reason and hope in the face of
hate.

Of standing up for transgender rights, for our being.

Of refusing to swear or allow name calling.

Of not always swearing six times when standing up.

Screw fibromyalgia, screw sciatic nerves and,

Screw transphobes, violence, and their wild, wilful
ignorance.

Today I am proud,

Of refusing to back down to prejudice,

To those who limit women to wombs, to blood.

Today I am proud,

Of Josephine Butler, Davison and Pankhurst,

Of Sylvia Rivera and Wendy Carlos.

Of Rosalind Franklin, of Jocelyn Bell Burnell,

Of Mary Wollstonecraft and Maya Angelou.

Of Ada Lovelace, Chicago, of Davis and Thunberg,

Of all the women who forced the world to change.

Of all the women we allowed to be forgotten,

And all those who keep up the fight.

Because we still, still live in a world where,

Women are imprisoned for their education,

And their uncovered hair.

Today I am proud,

Of the women I know.

The survivors, the thrivers, the wounded, the
abused.

Of the feminist spirits who refused all misuse.

The bruised, the artists, the musicians and poets,

And the ones who have not yet learned,

That every woman's voice is important.

Today I am proud,

Of all who signed # Me Too or spoke out for black lives.

Who need rape alarms, fisted keys and hands over drinks,
And yet are still blamed for being assaulted.
Call a friend, dress up bright, be seen,
Stick to main roads, dress humble, show no skin.
Be just like Sarah Everard when she was killed,
Or like I was when assaulted on a path,
I walked a thousand times before I allowed myself to be.
Today I am proud,
Of all who choose to give birth and who choose,
Not to give birth.
And those who mourn because they cannot choose.
Of the women who sang out **I Can't Keep Quiet**,
In city streets, who felt every word, who wept as they sang.
I'm proud of you all, high glass ceiling, low floor,
VAT on a tampon, wolf whistles, and pay gaps.
And everyday sexism if not every single damn hour.

I'm proud of you all for massed resilience stories,

That you only need because the world,

Treats you so fucking poorly.

Today I am proud,

To be a woman.

I am proud to be a woman.

Proud to be a woman.

Clare Matthews

Acknowledgements

Thank you for taking the time to read In the Footsteps of Walker Women. We hope it has entertained you, empowered you, and that you felt empathy with the wonderful stories.

All of the story holders are women who are us, could be us, or have been us. They are our neighbours, friends, grandmothers, mothers, daughters, and sisters. Women who have experienced universal challenges and achievements and whose stories may resonate with your own.

Thank you to the phenomenal, inspiring women in this book who opened their world to a stranger and allowed me the honour of hearing and retelling their journey. Thank you for your trust and honesty. Massive thanks to the magnificent team at Pottery Bank Community Centre, who commissioned Write on the Tyne to create such an important book and who always made me feel so welcome. The whole team and service are an exceptional asset to a community in need.

Thank you to the funders who allowed this project to happen – The National Lottery Heritage Fund and Community Foundation.

Special thanks to Leigh Burnarde who helped promote the project and much thanks to Ren, who granted permission to use lyrics from his song, "Hi Ren."

Profits from this book go to Pottery Bank Community Centre and Write on the Tyne – both are non-profit organisations supporting and giving opportunities to marginalised people.

If you have enjoyed this book, please leave a review on Amazon and Goodreads. Reviews help to boost the visibility of books to potential readers and also show appreciation for the story-holders and creatives involved in the many hours it takes to produce a book.

Helen Aitchison

For more information about Pottery Bank visit
www.potterybankcc.co.uk

For more information about Write on the Tyne visit
www.writeonthetyne.com